Dodd Alley

Gamers and Gorehounds

The Influence of Video Games on the Contemporary American Horror Film

VDM Verlag Dr. Müller

ISBN: 978-3-8364-12737-1

2

Table of Contents

Chapter 1: Introduction

A hallmark of popular culture is name recognition. Mario, Zelda, and Sonic the Hedgehog are just a few character names that have been recently cemented into popular culture. However, these names derive from a relatively new form of entertainment. They are not the names of characters from a popular blockbuster film, nor from a highly rated sitcom. They are not even characters from a best-selling novel. These are characters to whom people relate on an entirely different level from passive forms of entertainment such as film or television; audience members can essentially become these characters, explore their environments, and decide their fates. Mario, Zelda, and Sonic the Hedgehog are characters from popular video games.

In today's culture, it is difficult to be unfamiliar with video games. It is a form of new media that has initiated a craze in the entertainment industry. During the Christmas season of 2006, video games topped newspaper headlines as the newly-released Nintendo Wii and Playstation 3 home consoles disappeared from store shelves and became top-selling commodities. The demand for these new items was so high that the Wii and Playstation 3 were purchased at outrageous prices through sellers' markets and auction websites such as E-Bay. Millions of game-playing Americans were willing to brave the elements, wait in long lines, and invest hefty amounts of money just to possess the latest trend in video game technology.

It is quite evident that video game technology is becoming more present in American entertainment. Popular consoles are constantly being updated and released to provide more engaging and realistic experiences for their audiences. The realism is

4

introduced though the use of newer graphics that are photographic in nature, and by creating three-dimensional worlds which are so detailed that players could perceive them as actual reality. The realism and presence of video games have even been represented and embodied through the film medium, which will be discussed at great length in this study. However, in order to understand the pivotal role that video game technology plays in contemporary American society, it is first pertinent to comprehend how digital gaming began and how it has evolved into the influential industry that it is today.

Compared to the photorealistic graphical representations that are produced today for compact gaming systems, original digital games were primitive. *Spacewars* (1962), one of the first computer games, was a program that allowed two players to interactively manipulate images on a video screen. However, few people were able to enjoy *Spacewars*, as it required computers that were "the size of a small room or a large car."[1] These computers were only affordable for businesses with large budgets, rather than individual homes.

During the following decades video games evolved from esoteric experiments by programmers into an accepted part of mainstream entertainment. The 1970s and the 1980s opened the doors of American homes to video game technology. Atari's 2600 console was released in 1977 and "arguably became the first games console to be bought in significant numbers."[2] Money was spent by Americans on these consoles as well as in public video game arcades. While the Atari's popularity declined in the early 1980s, the personal computer became more affordable and abundant in homes. Developers saw the

---

[1] John Kirriemuir, "A History of Digital Games," <u>Understanding Digital Games</u>, Eds. Jason Rutter and Jo Bryce (Thousand Oaks, CA: Sage Publications, 2006) 22.
[2] Kirriemuir 24.

home computer as a platform for marketing video games. It was in the 1980s that "…the line between home computers and video games consoles became blurred; to this day, the phrases 'computer games' and 'video games' are often used interchangeably."[3]

From this point forward, video game technology had entered the domestic space and remains an integral part of that space today. After the decline of Atari, home consoles became popular once more with companies such as Nintendo and Sega creating top-selling units and game titles in the early 1990s. This eventually led to the development of portable systems such as the Nintendo Game Boy and Sega Game Gear, allowing trendy video games to be taken out of the home and enjoyed anywhere.

Video games have gone from expensive electronic experiments to affordable, everyday luxuries. Today, the technology is exhibited virtually everywhere from computer screens, to home televisions, to cellular phones. Companies such as Microsoft and Sony have noticed the profitability of digital gaming and have created some of the best-selling consoles on the market. On top of mobility and affordable pricing, video games continue to improve on aspects such as graphics and processing power. The technology has even proven to be legitimate competition against other entertainment outlets. Video games have permeated mainstream entertainment to the point of affecting and altering the way things are created and perceived. This includes the production of films.

With video games saturating American culture, it is no surprise that the interactive medium is reflected in film. While the vast majority of feature films are, of course, fictional narratives, they also rely on real life occurrences to play on the emotions

---

[3] Kirriemuir 26.

and knowledge of the audience. This could range from the depiction of a popular technology, to the representation of gender and race, to the demonstration of a political conflict or war. The inclusion of video game technology in film is inevitable because it is a popular idea recognized by contemporary, game-playing audiences.

The influence of gaming on film is not just affected specifically by video game technology, but also by the all-encompassing idea of new technology itself. It is important to first understand the ways in which one medium affects another with the improvement of technology. With constant innovations, technology has gradually insinuated itself more and more into everyday life as a part of an inevitable process of adaptation. When popular and successful technological breakthroughs are presented to the mainstream, consumers have little choice but to progress forward and adapt to these widely accepted ideas. The introduction and popularity of a single technological idea can greatly affect the routine activities and expectations of regular consumers because it achieves its known presence.

One of the reasons that technology has a widely-recognized presence is that one medium has the capability to coexist with another. As new media technologies continue to be produced, old ones do not go away. Instead they continue to thrive by being represented through other new and widely-accepted forms of media. Various theories have been constructed to explain this process. One concept that explains the progression of technology is remediation. This is defined as "...the formal logic by which new media refashion prior media forms."[4] Authors Jay Bolter and Richard Grusin define a medium as "that which remediates" and argue that:

> A medium in our culture can never operate in isolation, because it must enter into relationships of respect and rivalry with other media. There may be or may have been cultures in which a single form of representation (perhaps painting or song) exists with little or no reference to other media. Such isolation does not seem possible for us today, when we cannot even recognize the representational power of a medium except with reference to other media.[5]

It is in contemporary society that new mediums continue to thrive on the ideas of older ones.

One such example of a popular medium that coexists with older, pre-existing media is video games. The newer video game medium does utilize its unique interactive qualities. However, it many times relies on the older film medium as an inspiration for narrative elements or aesthetics. According to authors Geoff King and Tanya Krzywinska, the development of three-dimensional graphics and the technical ability to create more complex game worlds has "…led many games to aspire to a film-like quality of reproduction. Many also draw on narrative and generic frameworks familiar from the cinema."[6] Aspects of film including mise-en-scene, cinematography, and music are prevalent in many game titles and create an interactive movie to enhance the playing experience. The most prominent examples are film-based video game titles such as *The*

[4] Jay D. Bolter and Richard Grusin, Remediation: Understanding New Media, (Cambridge, MA: The MIT P, 1999) 273.
[5] Bolter and Grusin 65.
[6] Geoff King and Tanya Krzywinska. "Film Studies and Digital Games," Understanding Digital Games, Eds. Jason Rutter and Jo Bryce (Thousand Oaks, CA: Sage Publications, 2006) 115.

Godfather which recreate scenes from a popular film and put the player in control of the film's original narrative. While video games offer an interactive experience beyond that of the passive, film-viewing experience, many of them continue to coexist with the older film medium as a means of improving the gaming experience for the player.

Another reason for the widespread presence of technology is the convergence of different media forms. While similar to remediation, this convergence does not necessarily refer to the presence of older media in newer media outlets, but instead refers to all popular and new technologies working together in the contemporary landscape. This could include digital phone technologies being developed with computer capabilities, or portable music devices including the functions of a television. Companies that create new media technologies essentially fuse their ideas to better distribute information. *Convergence Culture* author Henry Jenkins further elaborates on this media convergence by saying:

> New media technologies enabled the same content to flow through many different channels and assume many different forms at the point of reception. At the same time, new patterns of cross-media ownership that began in the mid-1980's, during what we can now see as the first phase of a longer process of media concentration, were making it more desirable for companies to distribute content across those various channels rather than within a single media platform.[7]

An example of this content distribution though media convergence is the capability to play video games on a mobile phone. The characteristics of mobile technology are

---

[7] Henry Jenkins, Convergence Culture: Where Old and New Media Collide (New York: New York UP, 2006) 11.

combined with computer technology to create a hybrid that promotes game play, not just in the home or arcade, but anywhere in the world. Another example are I-Pod portable devices, which combine portable music technology with television allowing people to consume music, sitcoms, and news programs virtually anywhere.

Throughout cinematic history, film has relied on the previously-described processes of remediation and convergence as a means of succeeding with mainstream audiences. One prominent example is the invention of the television. In the early 1950s, television sets began to turn up in households across America. While movie theaters exhibited cartoons, newsreels and film features, audience members no longer saw the point in going out for entertainment when it was available at home. Programs on television began to pose a threat to production studios and movie theater owners.

To resolve this problem, Hollywood studios created television shows to earn a share of the profits from the successful television industry. Walt Disney, for example, signed a contract with ABC to produce the weekly series *Disneyland*. The show "permitted Disney to publicize his theatrical films and his new theme park. Disney filled his program with shorts and excerpts from the studio library. And, when one of his TV series struck a chord, a reedited version of the programs could be released as a profitable theatrical feature."[8] The film industry was not destroyed by the invention of the television. It "simply adjusted by expanding their activities to encompass both entertainment media."[9] Television and film eventually worked together to benefit both industries, even though they were initially competitors. The two mainstream outlets

[8] Kristin Thompson and David Bordwell, Film History: An Introduction, 2nd ed. (New York: McGraw Hill, 2003) 333.
[9] Thompson and Bordwell 333.

converged to bring big screen entertainment to the small screen, and sometimes vice versa. Today television and film work even closer together. Cable television is even a remediation of film as it keeps old, restored films alive through networks such as Turner Classic Movies and American Movie Classics.

Another new technology that affected the film industry was the invention of the Betamax video recorder and the Video Home System (VHS) in the late 1970s. Movie studios felt once again threatened as the possibility existed for people to record and view films from television instead of attending the movie theaters. However, the movie industry once again adjusted to the inevitable new technology and once again saw profit potential. According to film historians David Bordwell and Kristin Thompson, "Just as sales of films to broadcast television proved to be an unexpected blessing in the 1950's and 1960's, so movies on tape became another way for studios to earn still more money."[10] Instead of suffering from the impact of the new technology, film converged with home video to save the industry and appease viewers. Movie studios did so by establishing their own divisions to produce, market, and distribute films on videocassette for home viewing.[11] Theatrical ticket sales were not harmed as lucrative rental and purchase profits poured in.

Recently video game technology, like television, has posed a challenge for the film industry. In 2002, $10.3 billion was made in the United States on video game hardware, software, and accessories.[12] While these numbers are not yet lucrative enough

---

[10] Thompson and Bordwell 680.

[11] Thompson and Bordwell 680.

[12] Aphra Kerr, "The Business of Making Digital Games," Understanding Digital Games, Eds. Jason Rutter and Jo Bryce (Thousand Oaks, CA: Sage Publications, 2006) 38.

to surpass film industry profits, it has become a new and recognizable form of entertainment. Just as in the 1950s and the 1970s, the film medium has adjusted to the money-earning video game medium. Therefore, it is not surprising that films have acknowledged the presence of video game technology with their narratives.

It was previously discussed that video games are a remediation of film by utilizing both visual and narrative aspects of film. Specific studios have even allowed for films to be remade as videogame titles. Such game titles include *The Godfather* and *Enter the Matrix*, the latter of which served as a narrative extension of the *Matrix* films. The integration of the pre-existing film into the videogame medium is a recent trend and is an example of new media technology working in remediation with film. However, just as modern and interactive gaming technology has embraced cinema, the film medium has embraced video games. Unlike remediation, which involves the reliance of a newer medium upon an older one, the film medium is an older technology attempting to reflect on a newer technology as a means of relating to contemporary society and the people living in it. The inclusion of video game technology within film provides a crossover appeal that speaks to a generation of viewers familiar with the pervasive existence of the video games.

As the interactive appeal of video games has established itself and grown in popularity, film has responded to this craze. Digital games have become the focal point of interest in films of various genres since the early 1980s. One film genre that has particularly been affected by popular gaming is horror. This thesis is an analysis of horror films from 1990 to the present day that recognize the existence of the new video game technology, and incorporate it into their content. Before focusing on these specific horror films, it is imperative to recognize the existence of both video game-based films that were produced prior to 1990 and films not classified within the horror genre.

The first films to recognize are those which identified the existence of video games prior to 1990. The horror films in this study parallel the 1990s decade in video game history when consoles made by Sega and Nintendo were cultural staples which resulted in one of the largest and continuous booms in video game sales, to be further discussed in Chapter 2. However, prior to this period, video games were popular entities upon which film looked for source material. Some of these were not even considered horror titles like the films that will be discussed further in this study. With the establishment of the Atari home console, personal computer games, and video arcades, these films created fictitious accounts regarding the new, interactive medium.

One example is the science fiction film *The Last Starfighter* (1984), which follows a game-obsessed teenager who is recruited as a space fighter after playing an arcade game. The game itself is a recruiting tool that gauges the motor coordination of players to find the universe's next salvation. In this instance, the teenager's investment in the game catches the attention of a space scout and the teen is recruited by the Star League of Planets to fight enemies similar to those he has defeated within the arcade game. *The Last Starfighter* is one of the first films to depict the idea of video game consciousness which had begun to take shape in America.[13] The film implies human

---

[13] Vivian Sobchack, Screening Space: the American Science Fiction Film, 2nd ed. (New York City: Ungar Company, 1993) 224.

attachment to digital games and the focused, intense mindset that comes with playing these games.

Another example is the anthology film *Nightmares* (1983), which serves as a precursor to some of the more contemporary horror titles of this thesis. One particular segment in the film focuses on an arcade-dwelling teenager who, after fanatically playing a game, is sucked inside of it and becomes physically trapped inside the game as a punishment for his persistent foolishness. The film segment, titled "Bishop of Battle", is similar to *The Last Starfighter* in that it recognizes a growing fixation with video games. In the 1980s, these films hinted that interactive video game technology was encouraging American teenagers to become immersed in or distracted by their game-playing habits. This depiction of video game obsession would later resurface in the 1990s as gaming technology became more home-based, and became the focal interest point of many horror films, which will be discussed at greater length further into this study.

Another group of films, not to be confused with the titles of this study, are those that do not fall into the category of horror, such as the aforementioned *The Last Starfigher*. While the films of this thesis focus specifically on the horror genre, there have also been numerous non-horror films that have served as adaptations of popular video game titles. These are adaptation movies that recreate video game characters and environments on the big screen. One notable example of these adaptations is the film *Mortal Kombat*. Based on the top-selling violent fight game of the 1990s, *Mortal Kombat* (1995) served as an action-packed extension of the video game and became the source of supplemental storytelling for those familiar with the game. The film even recreated elaborately designed fight moves and death scenes, which were recognizable trademarks from the popular video game. Other films were released which also relied on the expectations and knowledge of video gamers. Like *Mortal Kombat*, these were action films that were adapted from popular video game titles. Examples include *Super Mario Brothers* (1993), *Double Dragon* (1994), and *Street Fighter* (1994). These films differ from the films in this thesis because they do not rely on horror conventions or horror-themed games to tell their stories. However, these films are also adaptations of popular video games, like many of the horror films to be analyzed in this study. The film adaptation of the horror video game and its relationship with video game devotees is something that will be further discussed in this thesis.

It has been addressed that two different types of video game films exist: those which recognize video games in the diegetic framework of their storylines, and those which reference them as source material in video game adaptations. The general idea of video games impacting the film medium is open for scrutiny and argumentation. It is probable that all video game-inspired films exhibit qualities which reference the current state of video game technology. These could be films released during any time period within any genre. However, the breadth of this study focuses only on horror films produced from 1990 to the present day. There are specific reasons for staying within these time and generic ranges.

The selection of 1990 to the present as a time span focuses on more recent film releases, and it is the significance of video games during this time period that make it an ideal topic of study. While video games were popular forms of entertainment prior to this time period, the 1990s began to see a transformation of popular technology in the face of video games. During the 1990s, game developers began to propel "new extremes of technical innovation, marketing intensity, and cultural audacity."[14] It is from that point forward that video games became part of a competitive industry which continues to prevail in today's entertainment world. Video game technology became a commodity force that had a successful effect on admirers of the interactive technology, and this had much to do with the move of video games from out of the arcade and into the domestic living space. The mounting presence of video games was represented in films throughout the 1990s and into the new millennium like never before, and it is the increased inclusion of games in a market saturated with this new technology that makes this period of time appropriate for this study.

Another commonality of the films in this thesis is that they are all horror films. Unlike many of the previously-mentioned video game-inspired films, which resort to conventions of the action or science fiction genre, films in this study rely on characteristics such as dread and terror which are most prevalent in horror movies. Video games such as *Super Mario Brothers* were being adapted into feature length films of various genres in the 1990s, as previously discussed in this chapter. These adaptations capitalized on popular, recognizable video game characters and storylines. However, the horror genre represented video game technology differently during this time period. Instead of adapting video games, these horror films told stories that represented video games as villains. It was not until the following decade that the horror genre began to

---

[14] Stephen Kline, Nick Dyer-Witheford, and Greig De Peuter, <u>Digital Play: the Interaction of Technology, Culture, and Marketing</u>, (Quebec: McGill-Queen's UP, 2003) 128.

adapt video games just as other genres had already done so throughout the 1990s. However, why horror films were distinctly negative towards video games during the 1990s and why they did not shift in content until the following decade will be the basis of this study. Other genres in the 1990s seemed to embrace video games, while horror films alternatively vilified them. The horror genre referenced video games more negatively than other genres, and this unique distinction makes horror films the ideal focus for this study. From 1990 to today, certain movie titles, which will be discussed in later chapters, have introduced video game elements into horror cinema, and there is a question as to why filmmakers chose to affiliate popular video game play with a genre renowned for frightening its viewers.

To comprehend why video games are crossed with the conventions of horror, one could reference numerous theories as to why horror films in general are manufactured and consumed by audiences. Author Noel Carroll argues that the appeal of horror stems from the viewer's curiosity in discovering the existence of fictitious monsters.[15] Another theorist, Linda Williams claims that horror serves as a text for viewers to vicariously experience a sense of pleasure or pain through the film's protagonists.[16] However, some of the most popular and simplest claims about horror are those that, according to author Andrew Tudor, "focus on clearly apparent thematic features of the horror films of particular periods, treating them as articulations of the felt social concerns of the time."[17]

---

[15] Noel Carroll, "Why Horror?," Horror: the Film Reader, Ed. Mark Jancovich (New York: Routledge, 2002) 40.

[16] Linda Williams, "Film Bodies: Gender, Genre, and Excess," Film Theory and Criticism: Introductory Readings, 5th ed. Eds. Leo Braudy and Marshall Cohen (New York: Oxford UP, 1999) 711.

[17] Andrew Tudor, "Why Horror? The Peculiar Pleasures of a Popular Genre," Horror: the Film Reader, Ed. Mark Jancovich (New York: Routledge, 2002) 50.

These articulations typically refer to large-scale national concerns such as deadly wars or rebellious movements.

It is these articulations that are most present in many of the video-game-based titles described in this study. Video games that were released and played from 1990 through the present did not evoke a mass hysteria equivalent to that of a deadly war as prior horror films have historically articulated. However, many of these films do evoke similar moods of anxiety and fear. These moods derive from the presence of video game technology within the diegetic worlds of the films. Considering the success and popularity of video games at the time of these films' releases, it is evident that the horror films discussed here are the articulations described by author Andrew Tudor. While other theories of horror may be applicable to these film titles, the films strongly embrace the idea of horror reflecting current American culture. The narratives of horror films may be intended to promote anything from psychoanalytic subtexts to discovering monstrous secrets. However, the films in this thesis are primarily reflections and expressions of a time in American history when viewers are presumably familiar with video game technology due to its wide presence.

The body of this thesis follows the release of horror films that were greatly affected by the continuous rise of the video game industry and the choices filmmakers made to address this change. It is divided into two chapters: one which discusses films released from 1990-2000, and another which discusses films released between 2000 and the present day which utilize different methods of integrating video games into horror than those of the prior decade. Chapter 2 analyzes video game-inspired horror films which depict video games existing in the diegetic spaces of the narratives. This includes the domestic spaces of the protagonists. These spaces are many times strikingly representative of current American culture, and the storylines of these films revolve around time periods that reflect the present day, or a possible bleak future. Characters in the films are represented as normal human beings, some of whom live in safe neighborhoods and work regular jobs. However, the routine activities in these settings are disrupted when video games are introduced into the lives of these characters. This technology brings with it a sudden change that sometimes makes it difficult for characters to distinguish between real worlds and game worlds.

The video games not only exist within the space of the narrative, but they are also depicted as antagonists. Video game technology is represented in these films as a destructive force that endangers the lives of the film's protagonists. The underestimation of these technologies leads to horrific outcomes. Rather than simply being an interactive toy, the video game dangerously immerses its players or is responsible for its users behaving erratically. Theories pertaining to technophobia and immersion relate to the films which depict a video game console as a dominant force that, over time, fuses with human subjects, or makes them prisoners in synthetic worlds.

The films of Chapter 2 will be referred to as representational video game films in that they represent contemporary video game technology within the diegesis, rather than embody them through adaptation. Representational title examples include *Freddy's Dead: The Final Nightmare* (1991), *The Lawnmower Man* (1992), *Arcade* (1993), and *Brainscan* (1994). *Freddy's Dead*'s release in 1991 gave it the distinction of being the first film to affiliate game consoles with horror during the rising popularity of Nintendo and Sega systems. It also exaggerates the dangers and consequences of prolonged game play. Films such as *Lawnmower Man* and *Arcade* further demonstrate this concern by capitalizing on the popularity of virtual reality technology. At the time, virtual reality was being introduced as a revolutionary way of merging the real world with synthetic worlds. These are films that generate the possibility of the human mind and body becoming trapped in these worlds. The film *Brainscan* also focuses on imprisonment within the game, but emphasizes more the correlation between game play and aggressive behavior. In this particular plot, the protagonist becomes invested in a game with the objective of killing in real life. Another film that represents gaming technology is *Existenz* (1999), which shows the most prevalent subtexts of human/technology fusion. This film portrays the coming together of reality and game world by depicting game consoles made of human flesh, and game players living each day unaware as to if they are in a synthetic world or in the real world.

The second part of this thesis will focus on films from 2002 to 2005, all of which are video game adaptations. There is a distinct shift in the content of video game horror films at the start of the new millennium where video game technology is no longer portrayed as an antagonist. In fact, it is not even included in the diegetic frame of the film. Unlike the previously mentioned examples that represent the act of gaming, these adaptation titles present narratives originally produced as game titles. This shift from game representation to adaptation signifies the filmmakers' response to the popularization of video games. After exhausting the fear of video game technology, filmmakers here wish to embrace it by fusing game aesthetics with film. These video game adaptations primarily look to survival horror and first person shooter game titles as inspiration. Chapter 3 defines these gaming subgenres and the effect they have had within specific horror film titles. There is also an emphasis on how video games and films rely on one another for inspiration. Gaming has successfully relied on filmic influences to produce intense titles such as *The Godfather* and the *Resident Evil* titles. However, the film titles in this thesis illustrate a shift in the opposite direction, by relying on gaming aesthetics and narratives. Some of these adaptations are even based on games that were originally inspired by film.

While horror film aesthetics are successfully translated into video games, the video game being adapted onto the screen has resulted in negative response from critics. Theatrical reviews for these films shed light on why the integration of gaming worlds into filmic worlds does not succeed. Poorly reviewed titles include *Resident Evil, House of the Dead,* and *Doom.* These filmmakers failed to understand that bringing video games to the big screen would result in dullness and frustration as opposed to the genuine excitement experienced while playing a video game. Without the aspect of interactivity, viewers are essentially left with a video game minus a controller.

Since 1990, video games have had a noticeable effect on the way certain horror films are produced. The next two chapters will explore this effect.

Chapter 2: Video Games to Die For

In the year 1990, video games were a hot commodity. Not since the success of

the Atari in the 1970s had home gaming consoles been considered a prominent staple in

American households. The Nintendo Entertainment System (NES) from Japan became a

"dominant market force" following its conception in the mid-1980s.[18] Due to its

affordability and "rapid contraction in Europe and the USA", the Nintendo name was

well-known.[19] The early 1990s also saw the rise of Japanese company Sega, which

competed with Nintendo for a hold on the home gaming market. Beginning with Sega's

popular console, Sega Genesis, and Nintendo's NES, the two companies vied for the

best-selling gaming console throughout the decade.

Popular home consoles were not the only new technologies contributing to

gaming culture in the 1990s. Personal computers had become more cost-efficient during

the 1980s and game developers jumped at the opportunity to produce software for the

machines. By 1990, "the line between home computers and video games consoles

became blurred."[20] Virtual reality (VR) technology had also caused hype amongst digital

gamers. By the beginning of the decade, VR technology consisted of "televisual goggles,

motion-sensitive gloves, and even whole suits" and was being promoted as both "a

practical high-tech tool for training, education, and entertainment and a vehicle for

---

[18] John Kirriemuir, "A History of Digital Games," Understanding Digital Games, Eds. Jason
Rutter and Jo Bryce (Thousand Oaks, CA: Sage Publications, 2006) 27.
[19] Kirriemuir 27.
[20] Kirriemuir 26.

consciousness-raising and self-transformation."[21] While it was an expensive technology

to own, virtual reality gaming began to take off in arcade settings.

With this new form of entertainment in high demand, video gaming had

inevitably affected the content of other media. Film is one source of entertainment

affected by the video game craze. With current technology being established within the

popular American mindset in the 1990s, films began to reference technological

movements due to their undeniable presence and effect on society, and video game

technology was one of these prominent movements. This impact that video game

popularity began to have on film content is like that of many films that have been

affected by current events. Many movies take the audience on escapist journeys through

fictional worlds, but they are also many times a reference to current society. Films can be

seen as "exponents of American culture, or windows into the national psyche."[22] In other

words, films are many times created as references to what Americans know or feel at that

time. One prominent example are the science fiction films of the 1950s which show

traces of an America plagued by the fear of Communist invasion. These movies were

obviously not exact reflections of America with their alien or monster-driven narratives,

but the anxiety felt by these films' main characters were the aforementioned windows

into the psyches of Communist-fearing Americans.

These traces of societal components in film include depictions of popular,

technological ideas that have become permanent staples in American society. Home

---

[21] Daniel Dinello, Technophobia!: Science Fiction Visions of Posthuman Technology (Austin, TX: University of Texas Press, 2005) 151.
[22] Robert C. Allen and Douglas Gomery, Film History: Theory and Practice (New York: Knopf, 1985) 158.

video gaming is one of these popular technologies, and it made an impact on films throughout the 1990s. At the beginning of this decade, Nintendo and Sega had established home video game play as a permanent fixture of pop culture that would only continue to improve over time. This video game explosion even worked its way into the diegetic framework of films with storylines about the relationship between protagonists and video games. However, these films also proved to be terrifying in nature. It was early in the 1990s that horror films began utilizing game technology in their narratives to parallel the landscape of popular digital gaming. These films did so by representing game technology as a potential threat.

The American horror film has gone through a historical shift from presenting monsters as external threats to presenting them as internally sourced. It has created monsters in various shapes and guises. These antagonists range from Frankenstein's grotesque monster, to the debonair Count Dracula, to a teenage girl possessed by Satan, to a haunted video game. While all of these horror film threats are different in appearance or personality, it is important to note the origins of these monsters. External horrors depicted an outsider that brought with it "imported evil" into the protagonists' lives.[23] Space aliens from 1950s invasion films are a perfect example. However, a change in the late 1960s saw the emergence of evil coming from within the protagonist's realm.[24] This internal horror particularly focused on the antagonist as a member of the family or a close-knit community. Examples include films such as *The Exorcist* and *The Omen* which represented the Vietnam-era disruption of the nuclear family.

---

[23] Gregory Waller, <u>American Horrors</u> (Chicago and Urbana: University of Illinois Press, 1987) 3.
[24] Waller 3.

As with the emergence of internal horror, the depiction of the horror film antagonist has evolved along with society. A prime example is the representation of technology as the monster. With technology making itself more abundant in homes across America, electronic media have been vilified in contemporary horror films. Part of this vilification represents the manner in which these new technologies are enjoyed and consumed by their users. Today, technology is more personalized and interactive for the consumer. Unlike the television and radio, which require passive consumption, new entertainment technology requires active participation and personal input. With its peripheral controllers that demand input from users, video gaming is a pivotal part of this new interactive movement. Not only is video game technology a part of people's lives, but people are also a component of that technology thanks to its interactive features which requires its audience to become deeply involved. This includes becoming a character in a video game, or even wearing a game console, such as with virtual reality systems.

Because of its intimate connection with humans, new video gaming technology became a popular antagonist within the diegetic framework of internal horror pictures between 1990 and 1999. Game-based films of the action genre, such as *Mortal Kombat* and *Super Mario Brothers* were released in this era and were adaptations of games. However, game-inspired horror films released in this era were different in that they represented the game console within the diegesis of the film as a source of evil rather than adapting video game source material for a narrative. This idea of the horror film featuring the video game itself is a projection of technophobia. A basic definition of technophobia is the fear of technology. It reflects on "the dramatic conflict between the techno-utopia promised by real-world scientists and the techno-dystopia predicted by science fiction."[25] The technophobic experience "serves as a warning for the future, countering cyber-hype and reflecting the real world of weaponized, religiously rationalized, and profit-fueled technology."[26]

Throughout the 1990s, video game participants were becoming immersed in their game play. It is this sense of focused game play that certain horror films saw as the next technophobic threat. According to author J.C. Herz, "What makes it [a video game] immersive is a world where no territory is off-limits, anything you see is fair game, and all your actions have consequences."[27] Gaming technology allows players to "identify with certain characters that find themselves facing opponents who want to kill them, want to prevent them from achieving some goal, or want to mislead them."[28] This character identification essentially means becoming the video game character through interactive controllers. Unlike radio, television, or film, users experience intense involvement through game play. With video game technology becoming a popular and standard means of entertainment, representational horror films chose to focus on this notion of immersion within their diegetic narratives. However, they depicted this as a negative, distracting and imprisoning quality, rather than a positive or cathartic one.

Another aspect of contemporary gaming that inspired these representational horror films is realism. Since the emergence of home game systems in the 1990s,

---

[25] Dinello 2.
[26] Dinello 2.
[27] As quoted in: Arthur A. Berger, <u>Video Games: a Popular Culture Phenomenon</u> (New Brunswick, NJ: Transaction, 2002) 9.
[28] Berger 17.

developers such as Nintendo, Sega, Sony, and Microsoft have focused on making the gaming experience as photorealistic in graphical detail as possible for the viewer while also making lucrative profits from video game sales. Author Andrew Darley comments on the progression of games throughout the 1990s, "The environments of these games are rendered in extraordinarily realistic detail, with naturalistic surface texture, dramatic lighting effects and subtle use of colour. Nowadays the majority of adversaries – monsters, zombies, aliens and so forth –are rendered and animated with the same high levels of surface accuracy and increasingly this is combined with a persuasive anthromorphism."[29] A representational video game horror film of the 1990s mainly focused on this realistic nature of video games as a component in blurring the line between the real world and the synthetic world, and wreaking terror on the lives of its users because of this confusion. The move from pixilated protagonists to neatly-rendered, human-like characters in video games was a renowned technological breakthrough. It was also something that the films of this study focused on as a potential threat to the human condition. Almost all of the representational films in this study do not depict video games as two-dimensional and distant from their users, but instead as a technology becoming so real and unmistakably lifelike that it has the capability to seep into real life.

The film titles in this chapter reflect upon video games as something that have become frighteningly real and immersive. However, the first title of interest from the early 1990s was released prior to the rise of more sophisticated graphics, but

---

[29] Andrew Darley, Visual Digital Culture: Surface Play and Spectacle in New Media Genres (New York: Routledge, 2000) 30.

demonstrated technophobic tendencies regarding the standard, two-dimensional home gaming system. *Freddy's Dead: The Final Nightmare* (1991) is the sixth installment in the *Nightmare on Elm Street* series and demonstrates the video gaming console as a murder weapon. This sequel follows deceased child murderer Freddy Kruger as he terrorizes and kills teenagers in their own nightmares. With the nightmare world refuting logical boundaries, Freddy resorts to creative methods in killing his victims. One method is transporting a game-obsessed, drug-using delinquent named Spencer into a two-dimensional video game world. Freddy proceeds to terrorize Spencer by putting him in the position of a video game character that is mercilessly beaten to death by another character resembling Freddy Kruger. Freddy himself sits on a couch and controls the actions of the Freddy look-alike through the use of a standard game controller and a special controller attached to his trademark glove that contains razor-sharp blades for fingers.

This particular scene from *Freddy's Dead* is making a comment about gaming culture in the early 1990s. Popular systems at the time, which included Sega Genesis and Super Nintendo, demonstrated similar two-dimensional graphics to the game depicted in this scene. Freddy's special controller on his glove is also a reflection of a Nintendo peripheral device known as the Power Glove that enabled gamers to play video games while wearing a glove with an attached controller. While referencing popular game technology at the time, which allowed viewers who were familiar with the game a visceral connection to the movie, this scene is also a commentary on video games. The victim, Spencer, is depicted as a marijuana-smoking slacker that builds pipe bombs and undermines authority. Spencer's death within the video game ironically reflects his way of life. His ignorance is attributed to giving up his mind to the world of video games. Therefore, the person that lives by the video game dies by the video game. His investment in gaming is so intense that he is transported into the video game itself, where he meets his demise. Spencer fails to recognize reality and is consumed by technology as a punishment.

This depiction of video gaming in *Freddy's Dead* was a response to up-and-coming technology at the time. The character Spencer happens to be a juvenile delinquent, but he is also representative of the American teenager in the era of digital game development. This is the same American teenager who has been "plugged in" to various media, which include video game consoles. Author Richard DeGrandpre commented on this technological distraction by stating, "...it's obvious that we [adults] are simply accommodating our children to a distracted way of life, rather than trying to reduce their distraction by, if you will, unplugging them."[30] What DeGrandpre said of children is applicable to Spencer, a teenager who is a victim to technological distraction. Spencer's father is even featured in the film as a careless and angry person who does not realize that removing video games from his son's life is a stepping stone towards better communication. The sense of anxiety from Spencer's death scene stemmed from the attitude of youth culture at the time of *Freddy's Dead*'s release. This was the attitude of undermining parental authority while being negatively affected and distracted by video games. Parents at this time were beginning to notice that children were neglecting

---

[30] Richard Degrandpre, <u>Digitopia: The Look of the New Digital You</u> (New York: AtRandom.Com Books, 2001) 121.

homework and avoiding social confrontation due to the video games.[31] Author Dmitri

Williams refers to this period of time as a "dystopic wave" which "highlighted fears of

video games' effects on values, attitudes and behaviour and a rise in the language of

addiction in game use."[32] *Freddy's Dead* may be another installment in the gory

Nightmare on Elm Street series that caters to fans, but it is also the first horror film of the

decade to provide a cautionary message about how distracting video games can be for

players. The death of Spencer is referential to a time when the desensitization of youth to

video games was only just beginning.

Following *Freddy's Dead,* representational films on gaming and horror began to

shift away from reflecting the two-dimensional graphics of Sega and Nintendo, and

instead began to focus on more advanced, recent, and lifelike aspects of the technology.

Virtual reality hardware had begun to appear in state-of-the-art arcades and allowed

participants to step into a game world through the use of virtual, first person goggles and

motion sensitive gloves. In the early 1990s virtual reality became known as a flashy

media phenomenon which had become ubiquitous due to its sudden appearance in video

arcades across the nation.[33] 1992 also saw the release of the first "first-person shooter"

through *Wolfenstein 3D,* which inspired many similar titles created to "intensify the

illusion of actual embodiment and with it the adrenaline rush of the kill-or-be-killed

situation."[34] This illusion was created by placing the player's perspective behind the eyes

---

[31] Peter H. Lewis, "The Summer Report: Ex Machina; Child's Play," The New York Times 6 Aug. 1989
[32] Dmitri Williams, "The Video Game Ligtning Rod: Constructions of a New Technology,
1970-2000," Information, Communication, &Society, Vol. 6, 2003: 523-550.
[33] Dinello 151.
[34] Stephen Kline, et al. Digital Play: the Interaction of Technology, Culture, and Marketing (Quebec:
McGill-Queen's UP, 2003) 144.

of the video game protagonist. Therefore, rather than just seeing the character, players had the opportunity to be the character and experience bloodshed from his or her viewpoint.

As opposed to *Freddy's Dead*, these films dealt with virtual reality technology as a threat throughout the entire narrative. The first example came in 1992 with *The Lawnmower Man*, which was the first film to capitalize on the new virtual reality technology in real life.[35] This science fiction/horror film focuses on a simple-minded gardener named Jobe who attracts the attention of a scientist. The scientist believes he can increase Jobe's intelligence by exposing him to specialized virtual reality environments and games. Jobe does become a smarter man, but also develops an aggressively unhealthy attachment to the virtual reality simulator. The film concludes with Jobe being consumed into the vividly-colored game world where he exists as a computer-animated being, while ceasing to exist as a human being in reality.

The Lawnmower Man, like *Freddy's Dead*, depicts a human experiencing fate at the hands of technology. Even though the scientist believes virtual reality can make Jobe smarter, the film counters this possibility. Not only is the video game world seen as threatening, but it is also portrayed as offering no benefit to humankind. Jobe's interactions with the game world mirror that of game playing in reality. Just as players obsessively become better at and more immersed in a particular game, Jobe becomes smarter and more infatuated with virtual reality. His devotion to the virtual reality

[35] Richard Harrington, rev. of *The Lawnmower Man*, The Washington Post 7 Mar. 1992, 12 Apr. 2007 <http://www.washingtonpost.com/wp-srv/style/longterm/movies/videos/thelawnmowermanrharrington_a0ab25.htm>.

console becomes so strong that he permanently becomes fused with the technology by leaving the real world and becoming part of the virtual world.

Compared to *Freddy's Dead*, which focuses a sequence of the film on digital immersion, *Lawnmower Man* focuses its entire plot on this concept. This different narrative focus is a suggestion of the coming of virtual reality technology at the time. New virtual reality technology provided a means of "…blocking as many of the senses as possible to the outside world and making it possible for the user to perceive only the artificial world, by the use of goggles, headphones, gloves, and so on."[36] With this new equipment requiring players to literally wear hardware, virtual reality technology was taking video gaming to a whole new level during this time period. *Lawnmower Man* is a film that utilizes this as a plot device as a means of keeping up with gaming in popular culture, yet, like *Freddy's Dead*, expresses fear at the unknown consequences of the growing technology. The game world turns Jobe into a virtual megalomaniac obsessed with world domination.[37] A sense of anxiety from Jobe's power trip is particularly touched upon in the film's ambiguous ending. After Jobe physically disappears into the virtual game world, it is initially assumed that his non-existence in reality renders the world a safe place. However, the film closes with every telephone across the world ringing as a result of Jobe becoming immersed, not just within the virtual reality console, but within global technology. The ending leaves the viewer with a feeling of uncertainty and anxiety that virtual reality consumes not just sensory perception, but the mind, body,

---

[36] Alison McMahan, "Immersion, Engagement, and Presence: a Method for Analyzing 3-D Video Games." The Video Game Theory Reader, Eds. Mark J. Wolf and Bernard Perron (New York: Routledge, 2003) 77.

[37] Geoff King, Spectacular Narratives: Hollywood in the Age of the Blockbuster (New York: I.B. Tauris, 2000) 190.

and soul. The essence of this fear was inspired by the real-life presence of virtual reality machines in arcades that appeared to be fun, but were still considered new and mysterious to gamers.[38] The idea of Jobe being consumed into a global information highway also suggests a sense of fear toward new computer and telecommunication technology in general. Therefore, *Lawnmower Man* capitalizes on negative side effects of these new technologies and extends to viewers the possibility that the new-fangled and mysterious virtual reality console may lead to unhealthy side effects in its participants. With video games literally becoming fused to the human body at this time, *Lawnmower Man* revolves around the popular, growing obsession with virtual reality and its synthetic worlds.

A similar example of virtual reality horror was demonstrated the following year in the straight-to video film *Arcade* (1993). This time the victims are a group of teenagers selected to test a new virtual reality gaming system. They are each given a console to take home and try out, but each of them vanishes, as they are taken from the real world and imprisoned inside the virtual world of the gaming console. This is a world characterized by colorful, synthetic landscapes, and animated creatures that serve as villainous obstacles. In the end, the remaining, non-imprisoned character, Alex, prevails by leaving reality and physically going inside of this game world where she uses an "extra life" power-up to overthrow the evil force within the game, and release her friends from virtual captivity.

Like *Lawnmower Man*, *Arcade* is about subjects becoming physically imprisoned inside the game, and the fearful atmosphere of the film references the emergence of new

---

[38] Andrew Pollack, "Tech Notes, All Aboard for Virtuality," The New York Times 5 Jan. 1992.

technology, which includes virtual reality technology in popular arcades. The characters are literally pulled into the game world and no longer exist in the real world. However, this story features a happy ending due to Alex's heroics. *Arcade* once again puts an emphasis on video games as a potential threat with no benefit to society. This is evident when the teen characters' overexcited obsession with testing the console leads them to imprisonment within the game world. Alex is the only character in the group that shows disdain for video games. Despite her gaming inexperience, it is her common sense and life skills that make her the true heroine. Alex goes into the game to save her friends rather than play for fun. Therefore, she recognizes the video game's motives, and considers her game play to be a life-saving mission. Because Alex does not lose touch with reality, she is able to save her friends from the shackles of interactive technology. The final shot shows Alex and her rescued friends socializing outdoors and cherishing real life after realizing the horrendous effects of prolonged video game play.

While *Arcade* was a straight-to-video release that did not reach theatrical audiences, it is still considered a crucial text in the depiction of new video game technology. With both home gaming consoles and virtual reality considered the new wave of interactive home entertainment in 1993, *Arcade* made an attempt at predicting future trends in video game availability and consumption. This was in the form of a virtual reality home console expected to be affordable and accessible to young gamers. In reality, the move from the depthless, two-dimensional game worlds of the NES and Sega Genesis to three-dimensional immersion was occurring at the time of *Arcade*'s release. *Arcade* was a reference to this technical innovation. However, like the

34

previously-mentioned titles, it referenced the potential negative effects of high immersion and sensory takeover from video games.

The following year, *Brainscan* (1994) took another approach to deadly virtual gaming. In response to the current technology, the film was released at "a time when America's curiosity with virtual reality is reaching a fever pitch."[39] While utilizing a first-person, virtual reality perspective, the premise does away with goggle and glove hardware, and takes a more psychological approach. The filmmakers even indicated at *Brainscan*'s time of release their non-affiliation with previous virtual reality films such as *The Lawnmower Man*. Producer Michael Roy stated, "I refused to look at any other virtual reality films before making *Brainscan*. We wanted to create our own world."[40]

The film follows protagonist Michael as he comes across a new computer game titled *Brainscan*, which gives players the opportunity to brutally murder someone. Once loaded, the game taps into Michael's psyche so he can play it in a hypnotic trance, and wander around photorealistic neighborhoods that are strikingly similar to his own. While invigorated by the intensity and reality of the game, Michael is alarmed to later discover that murders are actually occurring in real life. Michael believes he is playing within a game world that merely replicates real life, but *Brainscan* actually manipulates Michael into committing murders without him being fully aware of his actions.

The previous titles involving virtual reality simulators, such as *Arcade*, dealt with the characters becoming physically imprisoned by the video game. In *Brainscan*, Michael is hypnotized by the video game and commits the murders through a simulation

[39] Anthony P. Montesano, "CD-ROM 'Trickster' Treat: Brainscan," Cinefantastique 25 (1994): 48.
[40] As quoted in: Montesano 48.

similar to that of a virtual reality gaming experience. Like the previous titles, the film is, according to director John Flynn, saying that one can be consumed by the media.[41] However, Michael is never physically trapped inside of a game world. He is instead removed from reality mentally, while his physical form remains in the real world to kill people as a result from playing the game *Brainscan*. Michael is controlled by the video game without literally going inside of it. Therefore, this film touches more on the ways in which video games can affect real life, as opposed to the prior films which depict their subjects becoming trapped inside of a game world.

The fears depicted in *Brainscan*, like the other films explained in this chapter, are culturally relevant at a time when video games were continuing to have an effect on its players and remove them from reality. Film critic Roger Ebert even stated in his review for the film, that *Brainscan* is not interesting because of its plot or murders, but because of its "portrait of a teenage boy living at one remove from the world."[42] When Michael murders his own best friend and attempts to murder the girl next door, he is in a trance-like state due to his exposure to the violent video game. These scenes promote a sense of anxiety, and pose the question of what happens when a young person invests so much time in a video game that he or she can't distinguish the real world from the violent game world. *Brainscan* is indeed another commentary on vulnerable teenagers, but with an emphasis on their susceptibility to this violence. Michael is a video game aficionado obsessed with finding the most violent rush out of game play. Upon initially playing *Brainscan* he is delighted before realizing the seemingly harmless video game is affecting

---

[41] Montesano 48.

[42] Roger Ebert, Rev. of *Brainscan*, RogerEbert.com 22 Apr. 1994 12 Apr. 2007
<http://rogerebert.suntimes.com/apps/pbcs.dll/article?AID=/19940422/REVIEWS/404220303/1023>.

real human lives. The film's subtext is that overexposure to violent video games eventually seeps into the human mind, whether one is aware of it or not. The only way to fight it is to develop a full awareness of reality without video games. Michael does so at the film's conclusion by disposing of the game, and pursuing a relationship with his next-door neighbor.

It comes as no surprise that *Brainscan*'s 1994 release coincided with an explosion of video game violence in the United States. While the film depicts a teenager desensitized to popular and violent video games, best-selling games in the United States at the time of *Brainscan*'s theatrical release happened to be first-person simulations that glorified weaponry, killing, and gore. One striking example is the popularity of the video game *Doom*, which made nearly eight million dollars in revenue in 1994.[43] While 1992's *Wolfenstein 3D* had already popularized the first-person perspective and synthetic bloodshed, *Doom* took video games to a whole new level by encouraging players to destroy monsters in the most gruesome manner possible. With violence this detailed, "It was impossible now not to suspect that the depth and conviction of computer-generated illusions had entered an unprecedented dimension."[44] The imagery in video games was no longer pixilated and cartoon-like, but rather finely detailed to make characters and violence appear photorealistic in nature. This emphasis on gaming depth made titles such as *Doom* appear to be murderous simulators rather than innocent video games for children.

---

[43] Kline 146.
[44] Kline 145.

Doom inspired an ongoing trend of violent games which led to titles such as *Duke Nukem 3D*, *Quake*, and the *Grand Theft Auto* series. With graphic violence successfully prevailing in the video game industry, the release of *Brainscan* was quite timely. As *Brainscan* depicted a youth impacted by the extreme violence of video games, the film served as a precursor for real life controversy surrounding the effects that video games have on teenagers. *Doom* would later be blamed for influencing the shooters in the Columbine High School massacre of 1999. Game titles such as *Doom* introduced the masses to copious amounts of blood and gore when, prior to 1994, such detailed representations were not a part of mainstream game imagery. With this concern being widely present in the media, *Brainscan* joined the pantheon of films questioning the danger of video games and was well ahead of its time in raising the question of whether or not a video game can enable the imitation of dangerous or criminal activities despite simply being a simulation in the safe and consequence-free environment of a game world.[45]

Following the release of *Brainscan* in 1994, the representational video game horror film laid dormant until 1999. The lack of representational video game horror films was perhaps a sign that technophobic tendencies toward video games were beginning to subside in society. However, the topic of interactive video game horror depicted in titles such as *Lawnmower Man* and *Arcade* was revived in David Cronenberg's *Existenz* (1999). Previously mentioned films have shown humans attempting to fuse with video game worlds as closely as possible, but *Existenz* portrays the closest connection. The

---

[45] Steven Poole, <u>Trigger Happy: Videogames and the Entertainment Revolution</u> (New York: Arcade, 2000) 210.

premise has game developer Allegra Geller showcasing her new interactive game. Instead of the game's console being made of electronic parts, it is a pod containing living organs best described as "a sort of hybrid of a laptop and a fetal pig."[46] The peripheral is not a controller or virtual reality headset, but an umbilical-like cord that plugs into the player's nervous system through surgically implanted ports. Throughout the film, Allegra and a marketing executive named Ted dodge dangerous assassins to protect the gaming pod from falling into the wrong hands. They even plug into the virtual world of the pods to retrieve important information. However, the virtual worlds are strikingly similar in appearance to the real world, which confuses the main characters. The ironic twist at the conclusion of *Existenz* is that Ted and Allegra are not really who they appear to be, and their adventure is really part of yet another virtual reality game that they are testing for another game developer. However, upon returning to reality, the Ted and Allegra characters hold the developer at gunpoint leaving ambiguity as to whether or not they are still in a game world.

Existenz provides an evident technophobic stance toward video gaming. The gaming pods in the film represent a nightmarish premonition of interactive biotechnology. One striking example is the game pods made of flesh. After humans had dwelled on the obsession of human/video game fusion, technology essentially becomes biology. With its umbilical peripheral plugged into the nervous system, the console in *Existenz* became a living extension of the human body. Cronenberg commented on the idea, "It seemed to me that what people are really doing in computer and video games is

---

[46] Murray Pomerance, "Neither Here Nor There: *Existenz* as "Elevator Film," <u>Quarterly Review of Film and Video</u> 20 (2003): 1.

trying to get closer and closer to fusing themselves with the game. The idea that a game would plug into your nervous system made perfect sense to me..."[47]

In addition to the organic features of the gaming pods in *Existenz*, the film also, like the prior titles, comments on becoming immersed in the game world. This is evident when Allegra, Ted, and the characters they encounter all experience confusion because the game world is mentally blocking them from reality. The film is deliberately baffling for the viewer because it is hard to distinguish which environment is real, and which one is synthetic. The game-within-a-game-within-a-game layers presented in the conclusion show that game technology has become so overwhelmingly real that it is hard to distinguish between the actual and the virtual. Therefore, everyday life consists of trying to decipher whether or not one exists in *Existenz* or reality.

The confusion between reality and superficial worlds in *Existenz* is part of what author Murray Pomerance characterizes as an "elevator film."[48] These are films depicting characters that transport themselves to other parallel worlds that are often times easily confused with what is reality.[49] In the history of film, these alternate worlds can range from dream worlds as demonstrated in *The Wizard of Oz* (1939) to digital environments seen in *The Matrix* (1999). In *Existenz*, this other universe is within the game world. Pomerance comments on this virtual world as "exceptionally realistic even to the point of being commonplace. And this commenplaceness makes possible the thought that living in this world would be a conceivable equivalent to living in this one,

---

[47] As quoted in: Steve Keane, "From Hardware to Fleshware: Plugging into David Cronenberg's *EXistenZ*," ScreenPlay: Cinema/videogames/interfaces, Eds. Geoff King and Tanya Krzywinska (London: Wallflower Press, 2002) 150.

[48] Pomerance 2.

[49] Pomerance 2.

this present space in which we pay for our ticket and go to the movie theater to see this film."[50] While viewers experience the frustration of not knowing where one world ends and the other begins, they are empathizing with the frustrations of the protagonists. Unlike other elevator films that give both the protagonist and audience the relief of returning to the real world, *Existenz* keeps its characters imprisoned, and the audience uninformed. It is this sense of audience immersion and confusion that sets *Existenz* apart from the other films in this chapter. While film titles such as *Arcade* and *Brainscan* privilege the viewer with knowing that the protagonist characters are immersed in video games, *Existenz* does not offer such a privilege. Instead it tricks the viewer into believing that Allegra and Ted are jumping between virtual worlds and reality when they are, in fact, inside of another game world throughout the film. Like the characters in this chapter who have become immersed by video games, the audience themselves become immersed in *Existenz*.

As the final representational video game horror film of the 1990s, *Existenz* cleverly conveys to its audience that, after watching characters become victims to video game technology, they themselves have also been fooled by the blurred line between synthetic worlds and reality. *Existenz* was yet another film of its decade to reflect the mysterious and unknown side effects of video game technology, which was constantly changing and progressing. With Nintendo, Sony, and PC gaming contributing to the rise of popular gaming, the possibility of becoming lost through game play was still a reality as games were becoming more photorealistically lifelike, graphically detailed, and

---

[50] Pomerance 10.

interactively immersive for the player. *Existenz* is the final horror film of the decade to boldly represent video game technology and capitalize on its possible debilitating effects.

In analyzing films, one may find narratives that reference and reflect the time period in which they were produced. This includes films that reference the current state of technology. The titles previously discussed span from 1991 to 1999 and focus on the video game console as this current technology. At a time when gaming technology was on the rise, some of it was inevitably depicted in the diegetic framework of specific film titles. While some films in close proximity to this time period may shed a positive light on the new wave of gaming, these particular horror films represent gaming consoles as the antagonist and question the dangerous implications of this new technology. While new home game consoles and virtual reality were intended to be fun, they were also immersive and distracting for some players. The films in this chapter exaggeratingly emphasize this anxiety that beneath the appeal of video games there are negative side effects unbeknownst to many players. While these films came to an end in 1999 and gave way to films that represented video games positively, this did not mark an end to technophobic video game horror films. Between 1999 and 2006, the video game horror film eventually shifted in content, and instead began to utilize films as an outlet for adapting horror-themed video games, which will be discussed in the next chapter. However, in response to changing video game technology, the video game as the villain eventually returned in 2006 after temporarily lying dormant. This will be discussed further in Chapter 4.

Chapter 3: Adapting the Horror Video Game

At the turn of the millennium, video games had not lost their standing in popular culture. In fact, gaming had become a more popular form of entertainment, with new companies heading up the industry. Unlike the Sega and Nintendo, which targeted children as players, Sony and Microsoft took a different approach by marketing video games to grown-up players. Despite the release of the Nintendo Game Cube in 2001, Microsoft and Sony triumphed in console sales, with cutting-edge graphics and a variety of adult-themed games. Increased sales were due to not only newer, cutting-edge technology, but the capability to capture older-aged players. "Targeting twelve- to twenty-four-year-olds directly addressed a group with crucial disposable income, but it also appealed universally to all would-be seventeen-year-olds in the gaming world."[51] With grown-ups embracing video games, that interactive medium had become more widely-accepted as a customary form of entertainment rather than just a toy designed for children.

Another important influence in the video game industry was the rising popularity of Internet technology. As more and more people accepted game consoles or PC's into their homes, coincidentally Internet access also became a permanent domestic fixture. This allowed for PC games, and Playstation 2 and X-Box titles, to be played against other players on a video gaming network. In the book *Digital Play: The Interaction of Technology, Culture, and Marketing*, the authors comment on the Internet impacting these video games by saying "… networked play – the connection of the machines of two

---

[51] Stephen Kline, et al. Digital Play: the Interaction of Technology, Culture, and Marketing (Quebec: McGill-Queen's UP, 2003) 153.

or more players so that they compete or cooperate within a shared game world – has been a component of interactive gaming since its earliest days. But its large scale adoption represents a quantum leap in the nature of digital play. Instead of games simply connecting human *to* machine, they now also connect humans *through* machines; skills are tested against people rather than artificial intelligence."[52] Due to this introduction of Internet technology, gamers were brought closer together through player-to-player communication, and were no longer limited to relying on the game console as a computerized opponent.

The film titles discussed in Chapter 2 span from 1991 to 1999 and focus on the video game console as the enemy. These films were produced at a time when game players, in reality, were mostly reliant upon the artificial intelligence of a game console or computer. This connection that players had with video games, while having minimal contact with other humans, contributed to the fearful thrust of these films that vilified the gaming console; there was no connection to the outside world. Teenagers who had grown up with the normalcy of video game technology did not miss the outside connection. In fact, the target audience for video games during this period was the adolescent group.[53] It is no coincidence that the representational video game films of the 1990s also cast the avid game players as adolescents. As seen in more than half of these films, the victims are naïve teenagers overpowered by the artificial intelligence of the video game technology. With easily-swayable teenagers primarily consuming video games, these films referenced the possible corruption of youth culture.

---

[52] Kline 186.
[53] Kline 184.

After the year 2000, the video game horror film genre exhibited a shift in content from the negative representational video game horror films mentioned in Chapter 2 to adaptations of popular horror video games. This shift from films that depicted video games in a more negative light was in response to the changes in video game technology and its users. With a more diverse range of players participating and the gaming experience becoming more social through the availability of the Internet, home gaming extended beyond the walls of the domestic space and was becoming less of an internal threat; people were playing with and against people through the medium of the Internet as opposed to playing against a machine. However, home gaming systems continued to become more advanced, graphically detailed, and violent. Horror game titles were highly publicized as interactive experiences so finely detailed that they were terrifying, and these intense experiences appealed to gamers rather than scared them away. Video games were no longer mysterious and new technologies, but were familiar to players and becoming more embraced by them. It is this video game-encompassing attitude amongst players that coincided with the film industry's decision to change the way video game films were produced. In 2002, Hollywood decided to capitalize on this video game adrenaline rush with the horror genre. Instead of making horror films of people in battle against video games, the film industry decided to give horror game fans a cinematic experience to rival the gaming experience by making films that embody popular video games. These films, which are still being produced today, are all adaptations of video game source material, rather than films that represent a video game console within the diegetic framework of the film. Video games are embodied by the films, which create cinematic equivalents of the gaming experience. The sources of fear in these films are not video games, but are monsters inspired by original video game source material. This puts the terrifying emphasis on movie monsters typically found in standard horror subgenres, such as zombies and aliens, as opposed to positioning actual video game technology as the antagonist.

In translating a digital game to the big screen, these titles rely on the integration of aesthetics and narrative from their game counterparts to further enhance the viewing experience. The utilization of game narrative in the horror adaptation film is partially based on the acceptance of the video game medium as a cyberdrama, which emphasizes "the enactment of the story in the particular fictional space of the computer."[54] Many popular titles were not only about motor coordination and skill, but about becoming immersed in good storytelling. Author Janet Murray states, "A story has greater emphasis on plot; a game has greater emphasis on the actions of the player. But where the player is also the protagonist or the god of the story world, then player action and plot event begin to merge."[55] Murray describes the player's attachment to the game narrative as dramatic agency, which "requires that we script the interactor as well as the world, so that we know how to engage the world, and so that we build up the appropriate expectations."[56]

The adaptations discussed in this chapter relate to this idea of cyberdrama in that they involve players in the storyline of the game in addition to having them simply

---

[54] Janet Murray, "From Game-Story to Cyberdrama." First Person. Eds. Noah Wardrip-Fruin and Pat Harrigan (Cambridge, MA: The MIT P, 2004) 4.
[55] Murray 9.
[56] Murray 9.

controlling its characters. After real world game players became immersed in the narratives of popular video game titles, the film industry decided to capitalize on those particular video game storylines, similar to the way novels are adapted into movies. However, unlike novels, these video game storylines are what authors Thomas Elsaeasser and Warren Buckland refer to as writerly texts meaning the player/audience has the ability to determine the outcome of the storyline by interacting with it.[57] Specific horror game titles produced writerly narratives so captivating and suspenseful that gamers played on the basis of driving their characters through the storyline just to reach the climax of the narrative and the game. This inspired the production of films that served as live-action reenactments of the popular game storylines in response to the original game source material being a hit with players. However, unlike the previously-defined writerly characteristic of video games, these adaptation films were readerly texts meaning that their narratives had predetermined structures and outcomes.[58] While integrating certain settings, characters, or narrative aspects from the video game, they did not include the actual capability to interact with the medium like writerly texts.[59] These readerly adaptations also included sequel continuations of game narratives that picked up where video game narratives last left off to give players extra installments of their favorite game storylines.

Game aesthetics, in addition to narrative, are also a prominent characteristic of horror game adaptations. In fact, many horror video games discussed in this chapter

---

[57] Thomas Elsaesser and Warren Buckland, <u>Studying Contemporary American Film</u> (London: Arnold, 2002) 167.
[58] Elsaesser and Buckland 167.
[59] Elsaesser and Buckland 167.

originally looked to popular horror films as the inspiration for their gaming graphics. These games were, in a sense, interactive horror movies where players could control protagonists through terrifying obstacles, which was a different experience from simply viewing horror movies. Despite the similarities in aesthetics, there remains a marked difference between film and video games as forms of entertainment. Author Torben Grodal notes, "The film experience is basically a passive one. The input-driven nature of film makes it easy to cue strong passive emotions, including experiences of fate, and they may evoke a strong autonomic outlet, like crying. In contrast, video games are based on acting out the emotions, and the games may therefore even create some kind of catharsis."[60]

Some of the horror adaptation films discussed in this chapter attempt to combine the passive enjoyment of film and the interactive experience of gaming by creating an aesthetic that encompasses both. Specific filmmaking techniques strive to recreate video game aesthetics by means of a cinematic apparatus. This aesthetic consists of camera placements that, similar to video games, provides the viewer with either a first-person perspective or a rotating, close-up shot of the main character. This aesthetic even includes the insertion of actual video game footage into the film footage. Some of these techniques are, ironically, replicating games that initially looked to the film medium for visual inspiration. As certain horror games incorporate cinema, the cinema also incorporates gaming aesthetics that, in a sense, give audiences a video game without the controller. The audiences are thus able to experience a sense of gaming without even

---

[60] Torben Grodal, "Stories for Eye, Ear, and Muscles: Video Games, Media, and Embodied Experiences," The Video Game Theory Reader, Eds. Mark J. Wolf and Bernard Perron (New York: Routledge, 2003) 151.

playing the game. This is a viewing experience that embraced video game aesthetics by reaching out to fans of the interactive medium, and was Hollywood's way of capitalizing on the technophilic attitudes towards video games in America.

The horror video game adaptation films beginning in 2002 are all based on a particular game subgenre: survival horror. The survival horror game is "a game in which the player leads an individual character through an uncanny narrative and hostile environment where the odds are weighed decidedly against the avatar [protagonist]."[61] These consist of games that position the protagonist as a third-person or a first-person shooter. According to Richard Hand, the horror survival game genre is descended from *Night of the Living Dead,* from director George Romero.[62] The film depicts stranded humans forced to survive an impending horror in the form of zombies. As the narrative progresses, the audience empathizes with the surviving protagonists as they overcome obstacles and destroy zombies. Survival horror games focus on similar premises while allowing interactivity for the players. They also incorporate a mise-en-scene that is clearly influenced by the film style.[63] It is these cinematic elements that make survival horror games easy to translate to the big screen.

The first prominent example of the survival horror adaptation is *Resident Evil* (2002). The premise focuses on a band of survivors much like those in *Night of the Living Dead*, but these ones are trapped in an underground laboratory with a large number of virus-infected, flesh-eating zombies. The group must be practical with their

---

[61] Richard J.Hand, "Proliferating Horrors: Survival Horror and the Resident Evil Franchise," Horror Film: Creating and Marketing Fear, Ed. Steffen Hantke. (Jackson: University Press of Mississippi, 2004) 117.
[62] Hand 129.
[63] Hand 128.

limited tools and weaponry to fight off the zombies and make it to the surface uninfected.

The protagonist driving the plot is Alice, an agile amnesiac with skills in hand-to-hand

combat.

Resident Evil diverges from the film titles in Chapter 2 that portray video games

as evil, because it clearly pays homage to its original source material. This is particularly

evident in the translation of the narrative from the video game to cinema. The film's

narrative is an extension of the *Resident Evil* video game and aims to appeal to its fan

base. The premise is a cinematic recreation of the complex *Resident Evil* game narrative,

which was a contributing factor for the video game's success in addition to its

challenging puzzles and obstacles. The *Resident Evil* game series was largely popular

because of its "sophisticated narrative", which gave players "increased variety not just in

regard to different skills and abilities, but to plot sequences as well."[64] Since the

popularity of the game originally inspired the production of books which further

elaborated upon the plot of the *Resident Evil* game series, the *Resident Evil* film was an

inevitable response to fans in the game-playing universe.[65]

Resident Evil also uses video game aesthetics as a way to make the audience feel

as if they are playing the game for the duration of the film. The film's director Paul

Anderson said of the film's cinematographer David Johnson, "He…showed a great

appreciation for the game. Like, in the game, there are lots of overhead shots – signature

shots to the game – and we tried to recreate those, so he was looking for…ways to shoot

---

[64] Hand 118.
[65] Hand 129.

the movie in ways that resemble the game."[66] Indeed it is Anderson's intention to please the makers and players of the game.[67] The protagonist characters of the film, most of whom are sexually appealing like the characters in the game, kill zombies and appear to enjoy the experience. These scenes of zombie battle many times embody signature shots comparable to that of the video game. In one particular example, Alice fights a pack of undead Doberman Pinschers. The camera revolves around Alice like a third-person character, which is a signature technique commonly used in the *Resident Evil* video games. She survives the dogs by using a pistol that she conveniently finds on a dead person in an adjacent room. Close-up shots concentrate on each bullet as it is fired at the dogs as a way of taking inventory on the character's ammunition levels. Being that the *Resident Evil* games ask players to closely monitor their character's limited bullets, the close-up shots of these bullets is a way for viewers to, as in the video game, keep track of the protagonist's gun rounds. Players of the game would realize that running out of ammo means being without a weapon and desperately resorting to physical combat. This becomes the case for Alice as she encounters this predicament. Once her gun is empty, she utilizes a flying kick to destroy the final dog. A spontaneous snatch of rock/techno victory music plays at the end of this fight scene before Alice proceeds to the next room to take on new adversaries. This use of music is a reference to video games in general which commonly utilize upbeat music to give the player a feeling of accomplishment after overcoming obstacles. It is appropriate here as Alice completes one level and progresses to the next like a video game protagonist.

---

[66] As quoted in: Hand 132.
[67] Hand 131.

The goal of employing the video game aesthetic in the film is to evoke a sense of game play within the cinematic experience. While there is no choice to interact, Alice's battle is intended to give viewers the sense of excitement and victory they would experience while playing the game. Both the look of the film and the narrative are intended to provide a sense of familiarity for gamers, and not just serve as a horror film to please the general moviegoing audience. The *Resident Evil* game titles themselves function as interactive horror films, not just games. They carefully incorporate every crucial, formal aspect of horror cinema with the additional aspect of interactivity. Just as the *Resident Evil* games are an immersive hybridization of gaming and film which rely on cinematic conventions, the *Resident Evil* movie is similar by embodying aspects of the video games. The film recognizes the popularity and imminence of its video game predecessor and openly welcomes its characteristics to appease its gaming-friendly audience. *Resident Evil* is a product of Hollywood that, through its sophisticated narrative and video game-inspired aesthetics, embraces video game culture rather than shunning it.

The survival horror genre was again adapted in 2003 with the theatrical release of *House of the Dead*, based on a popular first-person arcade shooter game. Like *Resident Evil*, the game and the film focus on flesh-eating zombies. A group of teenagers travel to an ocean island to attend a much-touted rave. After hitching a boat ride from a grizzled sea captain named Kirk, they arrive on the island only to discover there is not a rave. All of the previous partiers had been attacked and turned into zombie creatures. The band of teenagers fights off the creatures with an ample supply of weapons that they conveniently discover. Each teen is killed until the conclusion when one male, Rudy, and one female, Alicia, are rescued safely from the island by a helicopter.

House of the Dead very blatantly introduces video game elements into the film through storytelling and direction. Like *Resident Evil*, the film narrative is similar to that of the game narrative. The group of teenagers goes from one locale to another on the island, and each site (e.g., an old house, an underground tunnel system) offers objectives and challenges for the characters. In one specific moment of *House of the Dead*, a character named Casper reaches the beach of the island where he spots Captain Kirk's boat in the ocean. The boat is full of explosives and weaponry, and it is Casper's objective to reach the boat. While swimming the ocean, he encounters ocean-dwelling zombies as obstacles and shoots them along the way. Just as the video game characters overthrow hordes of creatures in order to move from one distinct level/locale to the next, the film characters do the same to convey a feeling of progression and accomplishment with the viewers. The film is not a video game, but it does embody the game. This flow of events is intended to give the audience the feeling that they are watching a video game.

House of the Dead is a film that celebrates video game entertainment, and wholeheartedly welcomes fans of the games to revel in the cinematic experience of film/game integration. Upon starting the DVD of the film, the initial selection menu goes as far as including an "Insert Coin" message on the screen to give viewers the impression that they are about to play a game as opposed to view a film. Director Uwe Boll clarifies this on the commentary track by saying, "You want to show to the hardcore gamers that you really care about the property, and that you not only want to do a zombie movie and a gory horror movie. You want to do a video game-based zombie horror movie. I think [*House of the Dead*] is in all the [arcades] in North America. People are growing up with that game, and sitting there and shooting. This is the mood of the movie, basically, to what we want to bring onscreen."[68]

The most striking example of game integration is through the film's visuals. Like Alice's battle with zombie dogs in *Resident Evil*, there is an emphasis on slow motion. There is also the use of 360-degree camera movement so the viewers can study in detail the combat tactics utilized by the characters. This is also a technique commonly used in contemporary video games, particularly of the fighting genre, to let players analyze combat strategies in detail. It is as if the film asks the gaming audience to observe closely so they can utilize the same maneuvers when playing the game. Also, the film inserts actual footage from the *House of the Dead* video game. These shots are used in the fighting sequences between the teenagers and the zombies as a strong reminder that the film is game-based. This is the most transparent example of the film attempting to give audiences the sensation of viewing a movie and playing a game simultaneously.

The release of *House of the Dead* further established the idea that specific horror films adjusted to gaming culture as a means of attracting more viewers. According to authors Jay David Bolter and Richard Grusin, "…just as computer gamers seek to borrow the cachet of cinema by styling themselves as interactive film, so Hollywood cinema is trying to co-opt our culture's fascination with new media by using digital graphics to

---

[68] Uwe Boll, "Commentary Track," House of the Dead, Dir. Uwe Boll. Perf. Jonathan Cherry, Clint Howard, and Jurgen Prochnow. DVD. Artisan, 2003.

refashion traditional, linear films."[69] *House of the Dead* co-opted the use of digital video

game footage, inserting it into the linear narrative of the film, thereby ignoring traditional

standards of cinema. The cohesion of the film is interrupted by the insertion of actual

scenes from the *House of the Dead* video game, which violates the practice of exclusively

using film footage in the filmmaking medium. With *House of the Dead*, the insertion of

digital video game graphics and embodiment of the game narrative is a method of

converging film with other familiar media. In this particular case, that medium is video

game technology. Therefore, *House of the Dead* capitalizes on the video gaming

experience rather than going against it. Instead of competing with video game

entertainment, *House of the Dead* tries to re-create the experience of playing the same

game at home or in the arcade.

In opposition to the representational films of the 1990s that saw distraction,

immersion, and sensory takeover as negative outcomes of playing video games, *House of*

the Dead encompasses these characteristics. Its use of rapid editing, video game footage,

and cinematography that replicates scenes from the game make it evident that the film

takes a technophilic stance as opposed to a technophobic one. The fears and anxieties in

this film stem from the presence of zombie creatures rather than the existence of video

game technology. With the video game medium becoming a prominent staple in the

entertainment industry, *House of the Dead* is a horror film that encourages gamers to

embrace the attention-grabbing visuals of the game world rather than fear it.

---

[69] Jay D.Bolter and Richard Grusin, Remediation: Understanding New Media
(Cambridge, MA: The MIT P, 1999) 147.

Following the release of *House of the Dead* in 2003, video game horror films

were absent from the big screen until 2004. *Resident Evil: Apocalypse* was released as a

sequel to *Resident Evil* in 2004 and employed similar game/film hybridizations.

However, in 2005, another adaptation of a popular game was released that established its

director as an auteur of video game-friendly pictures, as well as establishing familiar

conventions for game aficionados. Uwe Boll, the director of *House of the Dead*, filmed

another survival horror video game adaptation based on the Atari title *Alone in the Dark*

(2005). The storyline follows paranormal detective Edward Carnby as he discovers a

sinister plot to unleash deadly ancient creatures and open up a gate to an evil dimension,

which could result in the end of the world. Carnby and his archeologist side kick/love

interest set out to destroy these creatures while solving the mystery of their origins.

The plot of *Alone in the Dark* is based on elements of the popular video game

series, but it does not serve as a direct adaptation of game series' storyline. Released in

1993, the original *Alone in the Dark* video game is regarded by some as "the first survival

horror computer game."[70] Its "Lovecraftian" narrative proved to be a success with

gaming fans and inspired the release of sequels up until 2001.[71] Rather than taking the

plot of a pre-existing game and using it as the basis for the film's screenplay, the film

Alone in the Dark follows game protagonist Edward Carnby through a new adventure

that serves as a follow-up to the most recent game series installment, *Alone in the Dark:*

The New Nightmare (2001).

---

[70] Hand 117.
[71] Hand 117.

While the continuation of the game series' storyline in the film is a benefit for fans of the video game, it does not require all audience members to have some familiarity with the game narrative. However, *Alone in the Dark* is a film intended to cater to the growing fan base of the video game medium. *Alone in the Dark* screenwriter Elan Mastai says of the film, "I think games are a great source material for movies because [it] provides a really deep background for the character, and what's great about a game is that when you are playing you actually *are* the character. So there is that connection with the hero."[72] Director Uwe Boll also states, "….video game movies are like movies with the new bestseller. The bestsellers of the new generation are video games and not books anymore."[73] Just as literary adaptations attempt to attract readers into the movie theater, *Alone in the Dark* attempts to attract gamers by further developing a character and a storyline from the popular *Alone in the Dark* video game series. This is a strategy that attracts fans of the game, and those who, after actually playing the character Edward Carnby in the game, feel closely connected to his experiences and wish to become part of his further discoveries in the film.

The aesthetics of *Alone in the Dark* are also reliant on the video game medium as source material. While much of the film generically serves as a mystery, it eventually gives way to video game influences with the introduction of computer-generated creatures. The protagonist characters' constant "point and shoot" defense mechanisms against alien beings follow the template of video game narration by making the human

---

[72] Elan Mastai, "Into the Dark: Behind the Scenes of *Alone in the Dark*," <u>Alone in the Dark</u> Dir. Uwe Boll. Perf. Christian Slater, Tara Reid, and Stephen Dorff. DVD. Lion's Gate Films, 2005.
[73] Uwe Boll, "Into the Dark: Behind the Scenes of *Alone in the Dark*," <u>Alone in the Dark</u> Dir. Uwe Boll. Perf. Christian Slater, Tara Reid, and Stephen Dorff. DVD. Lion's Gate Films, 2005.

characters almost resemble game players using gun-like controllers. This is a distinctive visual trait that plays on the conventions of popular video games. One particular scene that exhibits this visual trait is one that pits Edward Carnby and his anthropologist love interest Aline against a barrage of dangerous monsters. The storyline instantly shifts from a horror/mystery to a flashy action film. Edward and Aline do battle with the creatures in a dark room where their gunfire creates a strobe light effect, while the camera shots cut rapidly between the protagonists shooting and monsters being slaughtered. Some of these cuts even position the camera in the first-person perspective of Edward or Aline as the creatures meet their demises. This sudden visual overload exhibits characteristics commonly seen in video games. The superfluous use of strobe light effects, quick cuts, and first-person camera angles do not just try to create a standard film sequence, but a sequence that evokes adrenaline and excitement with avid gamers.

2005's *Doom* is another notable release that attempts to enthrall viewers with its gaming integration. Based on a popular horror first-person shooter game of the same title, the film follows a squad of Marines that travel to the planet Mars to investigate possible distress signals coming from a research outpost. When they arrive, they find that mutant space creatures have overrun the outpost and are on the prowl for victims. The Marines explore the corridors of the outpost and diminish in numbers until the conclusion when two survivors manage to detonate the outpost and escape.

This adaptation is a clear homage to its original gaming source, and brings many elements of the game into the film. The plot of the film is an ongoing exploration of the outpost. With little emphasis on character development and story, *Doom* is in essence a video game with human actors. The Marines, while looking for a way out, repeatedly encounter mutants around each corner. This results in either the mutant being killed with a potent weapon, or the mutant destroying a Marine. *Doom* also maintains close ties with the game by introducing weapons affiliated with the game. However, the film also utilizes proper cinematography to make one sequence replicate the first-person aesthetic of the *Doom* survivalist video game. When one of the Marines, John Grimm, goes on a macho rampage to destroy the mutants, the camera takes a first-person stance from Grimm's perspective. This camera technique takes the audience down corridors where monsters appear everywhere. With the barrel of a gun placed at the bottom of the screen in first-person style, Grimm shoots every creature he encounters. When Grimm wishes to kill a creature with a chainsaw, the camera moves forward over a discarded chainsaw on the ground. Immediately, the weapon displayed at the bottom of the screen in Grimm's first-person position is a chainsaw. This method of switching between weapons found at random is another cinematography technique that matches the visual traits of the video game.

This particular scene, along with other direction and scripting choices, make it clear that *Doom* is a horror film catering to the video game audience. It does so by relying on the conventions of the first-person shooter video game. Author Sue Morris states, "First-person point-of-view is used very successfully in games to create a sense of the player's embodiment within the game space, and is recognized by game designers as contributing to a more visceral game experience because of the sense of immersion created. If primary identification is the cinematic subject's identification with the act of looking, then the [first-person shooter] player is unequivocally the one doing the looking."[74] The use of this first-person aesthetic is intended to fully embrace the audience, particularly those familiar with gaming. The film wants viewers to feel the excitement of gaming through a cinematic medium. *Doom* is a glorification of the video gaming medium and embodies the concept of the first-person aesthetic into the world of the film.

The aforementioned video game adaptation films serve as extensions and enhancements of the gaming experience. Instead of using the horror genre to make technology look evil, they strive to promote a sense of excitement in the audience equivalent to that of playing a video game. However, whether these films actually succeed in providing viewers with an equally rewarding experience is questionable. Author Tanya Krzywinska states that horror films and horror video games are different because films are enjoyed passively and the audience has a feeling of being a helpless outsider who cannot participate in the film.[75] The horror film "plays more overtly with the viewer's inability to affect the action..."[76] The films included in this study whole-heartedly embrace video game technology and strive to please avid gamers through their narratives and aesthetics. However, many filmgoers and critics seemed to agree more with Krzywinska's distinction between horror film and game; instead of becoming enthralled by the experimental merging of video games into the film medium, they showed their disapproval at the box office. Most of the films analyzed in this chapter

---

[74]Sue Morris, "First-Person Shooters: the Game Apparatus," Screenplay: Cinema/Videogames/Interfaces, Eds. Geoff King and Tanya Krzywinska (London: Wallflower P, 2002) 89.
[75] Tanya Krzywinska, "Hands-On Horror," ScreenPlay: Cinema/videogames/interfaces, Eds. Geoff King and Tanya Krzywinska (London: Wallflower Press, 2002) 216.
[76] Krzywinska 216.

failed both critically and financially with American audiences, demonstrating that
Hollywood has not been able to fully capitalize on the integration of video game and film
aesthetics, at least for audiences in the theaters.

Upon the theatrical releases of the survival horror adaptations, critics came to a
consensus that the employment of video game elements within film only leads to
frustration. Roger Ebert of the <u>Chicago Sun Times</u> stated, "*Doom* is like some kid came
over and is using your computer and won't let you play."[77] Other critics agreed with
Ebert that watching a video game without the freedom to interact was a useless principle
to incorporate into a film. Other previously-mentioned video game adaptation films also
opened to harsh reviews, particularly the features directed by Uwe Boll. Both *Alone in
the Dark* and *House of the Dead* were criticized for being poorly produced. However,
Dead was particularly criticized for its insertion of video game footage for the same
reason that *Doom* was criticized: people do not want to go to the movie theater to watch
a video game. Scott Brown of <u>Entertainment Weekly</u> wrote of the inserted game footage
in *House of the Dead*, "I'd call this lazy filmmaking, but that would imply the existence
of filmmaking here."[78] Brown's scathing review of Boll's movie illustrates this
frustration felt by film critics.

While film production companies between 2002 and 2005 were trying to build
upon the popularity of gaming consoles by releasing adaptations that embodied
survivalist horror games, these films were just as poorly received by audiences as they

---

[77] Roger Ebert, "Doom," <u>RogerEbert.com.</u> 21 Oct. 2005. 20 May 2006
<http://rogerebert.suntimes.com/apps/pbcs.dll/article?AID=/20051020/REVIEWS/51012003/1023>.
[78] Scott Brown, "House of the Dead," <u>Entertainment Weekly.</u> 10 Oct. 2003. 20 May 2006
<http://www.ew.com/ew/article/review/movie/0,6115,485226~1~0~houseofdead,00.html>.

were by critics. With the exception of the *Resident Evil* films, the video game adaptation horror films were disappointments in the box office. However, despite not being attacked so much by moviegoers, the *Resident Evil* films were still attacked by critics for their over-reliance on video games. It is likely that all of these films reached a niche audience of game enthusiasts, but the conversion of video game narrative into the horror film narrative clearly raised questions about general audience satisfaction.

It is common for horror films to look to the real world for ideas on what could be deemed terrifying. From 2002 to 2005, the horror film industry turned to video game technology for ideas. However, they did not vilify the technology as an impending threat. Instead the film industry recognized the video game as a growing medium that was becoming more and more accepted by the masses. Relying on the likelihood that general audiences would no longer find the idea of video games as a threat appealing, certain horror films attempted to embody the aesthetic and narrative components that made video game participation so appealing. The films discussed in this chapter were adapted from pre-established video game titles. They strove to attract avid video game players just as literary novel adaptations strove to attract avid readers. It is this model of technophilic adaptation horror films that has reached out to video game-friendly audiences since the beginning of the new millennium and continues to do so today.

Chapter 4: Conclusion

The previous chapters have analyzed horror films released during the past two decades that were influenced by the presence of video game technology in popular culture. Chapter 1 provides an introduction to the history of video games, how they have influenced the film medium, and particularly why they work well in the horror film genre. Chapter 2 explores films released in the 1990s that represented video game technology as a villainous threat to humankind. The attitudes towards video games in these films were fearful in nature because the interactive medium was depicted as a new technology with unforeseen effects on its users. These titles paralleled the unveiling of various video game technologies throughout the 1990s, which were ubiquitous and mysterious to users just like the games depicted in the films. Finally, Chapter 3 analyzes horror films released from the year 2000 to the present which, unlike the films in Chapter 2, are adaptations of horror video game titles that fully embrace the existence of video game technology. As a result of video games becoming more widely accepted by American society, these films embodied the substance and style of video games to appeal to a more technophilic audience. The adaptation films no longer relied on the audience's fear of video games, but instead on their love of the technology. The current chapter concludes this study by focusing on the recent presence of game-inspired horror films. While Chapter 2 identifies a group of game-fearing films and Chapter 3 identifies a separate group of game-friendly films, this chapter addresses a mixture of both. After the release of *Doom* in 2005, the streak of adaptation films was broken in 2006 with the release of a techophobic video game film similar to that of the representational video game films discussed in Chapter 2 that vilified video games within their diegetic narratives. The year 2006 saw the release of three films that were a combination of one technophobic and two technophilic video game films, and it is pertinent to address the presence of video game technology in these titles. These three films which were released theatrically in 2006 were *Stay Alive*, *Bloodrayne*, and *Silent Hill*.

The first of these films, *Stay Alive*, is mentionable because it is a film relating to video game technology like every other film in this entire study. However, this title is particularly noteworthy because it breaks the chain of titles that began with *Resident Evil* in 2002, and resorts back to the technophobic mood conveyed through the films of the 1990s discussed in Chapter 2. The film is not an adaptation video game title, but instead vilifies the modern game console as an unstoppable force with which to be reckoned in the diegesis. *Stay Alive* portrays video game technology as something to fear, but also capitalizes on the presence of recent trends and technologies in gaming, which will be argued further in this chapter. The film follows young Hutch who plays video games religiously with his tech-savvy friends. Much of the time these friends do not gather together to play in person, but alone in their respective domestic spaces, taking advantage of the availability of online gaming. When one of Hutch's gaming buddies turns up dead, he discovers in the deceased's possession a mysterious title known as *Stay Alive*. He distributes the game to his eager friends, only to find that they too begin turning up dead. The cause of death turns out to be related to playing the mysterious game. When Hutch's friends die in the video game, they die the same death in real life. This is due to a curse placed on the game by the ghost of a vengeful noblewoman known as the Blood

Countess. Hutch's peers continue playing *Stay Alive* and take for granted the possibility of death in the game world affecting the real world. Hutch, knowing the deadly effects of the game, takes it upon himself to prevent *Stay Alive* and the Blood Countess from killing not just his friends, but any other game player who may take the game into his or her possession.

Like the films of the 1990s, *Stay Alive* shows a darker, pessimistic attitude toward video game technology. However, in contrast with these earlier films, *Stay Alive* exhibits traces of contemporary video game technology that had improved and changed since the prior decade. In late 2005, the X-Box 360 was released as an update of Microsoft's original X-Box console. Even more so than its predecessor, the new console encouraged Internet access. While the system came equipped with the proper Internet technology and a premium connection service called X-Box Live, it also came with microphone headsets allowing long distance gamers to communicate with one another verbally. Along with X-Box 360, the year 2006 saw the release of the Sony Playstation 3 and the Nintendo Wii, which also encouraged Internet gaming. Personal computers with Internet access could also handle multi-player software for online gaming. Because of the availability of Internet access, popular gaming platforms at the time such as X-Box 360 and home computers gave players the capability to compete against others without meeting in person to do so.

Stay Alive's production coincided with the unveiling and release of these popular consoles. Unlike the films in the 1990s it places more emphasis on the capability of players to utilize Internet technology in their game play. With the popular consoles at the

65

time allowing more and more players to go online rather than meet with others face-to-face, *Stay Alive* depicts game players as solitary and capitalizes on moods of technophobia and anxiety toward video games. While the technophobic titles from Chapter 2 dealt with players being physically or mentally trapped inside video game worlds, *Stay Alive* focuses more on the video game world spilling into reality and how these video games can be transmitted between players at rapid rates. The film not only deals with Hutch trying to prevent the game, which has invaded reality, from killing his friends, but also trying to prevent the game from being distributed into the hands of others. Even after Hutch informs his friends about the dangerous video game, the ghost of the Blood Countess still sees to it that the cursed game ends up being distributed to and played by other unsuspecting gamers.

In apparent reference to the popular consoles of 2006 equipped to handle Internet game play, *Stay Alive* depicts the murderous video game as something that cannot be stopped due to the transmission of information made possible by the Internet. This is especially made evident in the conclusion of the film. After Hutch and his surviving friends defeat the Blood Countess and destroy the game, the story does not end happily. Despite overthrowing the one copy of the video game that threatened his friends, it is revealed that the Blood Countess already distributed multiple copies of the game. The film closes with *Stay Alive* being packed and distributed to video game stores across the world while teenagers excitedly await the release of the new game.

This conclusion is certainly a grim one that looks at video games and the distribution of digital information as the inevitable end of humanity. *Stay Alive*'s storyline of death in the video game influencing death in real life may be inspired by the issue of video games affecting the action of youths in reality. However, the real threat here is the deadly game's ability to reach players quickly before the protagonists can intervene. *Stay Alive* references a time period when games no longer have to be exchanged as tangible copies, but can be quickly delivered via an Internet connection. It also references a new era of game play in which players are no longer required to leave their homes to compete, but can play home alone thanks to an Internet connection. *Stay Alive* ends unhappily and ambiguously, and leaves a lingering feeling of anxiety that, thanks to the availability of broadband technology, video games continue to negatively affect young people by reaching them at rates more rapidly than prior years.

Stay Alive was the first film since the 1990s decade to depict video game technology as a possible threat to its players. However, in the year 2006, *Stay Alive* was outnumbered distribution-wise by video game adaptations which continued the trend of the films discussed in Chapter 3. These titles were *Bloodrayne* and *Silent Hill*. With *Bloodrayne*, director Uwe Boll, better known for helming *House of the Dead* and *Alone in the Dark*, continued to build upon his reputation as a video game adaptation auteur with the film *Bloodrayne*. Just as in Boll's prior films, *Bloodrayne* is reliant on an audience familiar with the video game. The storyline of *Bloodrayne* follows title character Rayne, who is a hybrid of human and vampire. Rayne is prisoner to a traveling carnival that exploits her vampire capabilities to withstand fatal flesh wounds. However, she manages to escape her captors. With the assistance of a group of vampire hunters,

Rayne sets out on a vengeance mission to destroy her father, Kagen, King of the Vampires, who long ago raped and murdered her mother.

Like Boll's previous work, *Alone in the Dark*, *Bloodrayne* takes familiar characters from a video game and places them in new storylines for game fans to experience for the first time. Unlike the original video game, which dealt with Rayne fighting Nazis during the World War II era, the film places the character in Medieval times. It also pits Rayne against her father Kagen, another character who is mentioned in the video game's back story. By utilizing these characters, it gives admirers of the video game a chance to bring their existing knowledge to the viewing experience, and enjoy seeing their favorite characters in a storyline never before presented in the video game.

Unlike Uwe Boll's prior film, *House of the Dead*, which, as discussed in Chapter 3, placed blatant insertions of the original video game into the film, *Bloodrayne* is more similar to Boll's *Alone in the Dark* by not relying on such obvious editing techniques. However, *Bloodrayne* still exhibits characteristics that cross over from the original video game source material. Boston Globe film critic Wesley Morris points out the film's comparison to the video game by indicating, "If [Rayne]'s journey's success seems contingent on tracking down certain power-boosting talismans (she drinks blood like Gatorade), it's because *Bloodrayne* is based on a video game."[79] The premise of the *Bloodrayne* video game shows Rayne attacking enemies, then drinking their blood as power boosters to help continue her mission. The film uses this same aspect of the video game as a means of forwarding the narrative. Just like the video game, Rayne must seek

[79] Wesley Morris, "'Bloodrayne' Fun Comes in Spurts," Boston Globe 7 Jan. 2006, 8 April 2007 <http://www.boston.com/ae/movies/articles/2006/01/07/bloodrayne_fun_comes_in_spurts/>.

out relics and drink her enemy's blood as a means of survival. This takes to her to the final boss, Kragen, who she must defeat before the film's end. The film *Bloodrayne* looks to the video game for both storyline and the main character's motivation to progress through this storyline. This includes its utilization of pre-existing characters from the video game and its inclusion of confrontations that reward the character with energy-boosting power-ups. The result is a movie that stays true to its video game inspiration for the sake of pleasing fans.

Bloodrayne is not the only film in 2006 to show admiration of its video game source. *Silent Hill* is another horror film released the same year that is based on a popular video game. *Silent Hill* follows Rose as she finds herself mysteriously lost in the title's small locale. After her daughter turns up missing, she journeys further into the town only to discover dark secrets. Beneath the ghost town's abandoned buildings are a wide range of monstrous figures including murderous nurses and a torturer with spikes for hands. It is up to Rose to find her daughter while also figuring out how to escape the hellish town of Silent Hill. Like the adaptations discussed in Chapter 3, *Silent Hill* is a video game adaptation film that pays homage to the video game's content and its aesthetics. The film's devotion to the video game is most evident in its plot. The premise of the film is strikingly similar to that of the video game, with the exception of a male protagonist being trapped in Silent Hill. The film also brings enemies from the video game, including the aforementioned spike-handed torturer, and pits them against Rose during her struggles. However, the storyline is confusing because it relies on conventions used in the game that perhaps only a player could understand. An example of this is when

69

Rose is alerted of the presence of nearby enemies by a mysterious town siren. This is
also the method of warning the player of impending enemies in the original video game.
While audiences unfamiliar with the game may not realize what the sounding of the
town's siren means, fans of the game may revel in the anticipation of approaching
monsters. *Silent Hill* made a #1 debut in the box office and likely attracted general
audiences, but the film is clearly made for its video game fans. Critic Roger Ebert
deduces from his confusion over the film that those who have played the game will likely
be the ones to understand it and enjoy it.[80] With its commitment to the game's plotline
and visuals, *Silent Hill* is clearly a film that celebrates the video game's famed
creepiness, and especially reaches out to gamers as a means of reliving the gaming
experience in a cinematic setting. Like the films of Chapter 3, this is a film that
embodies its source material and recognizes the contemporary, movie-going audience's
familiarity with popular video game titles.

While *Bloodrayne* and *Silent Hill* continued the trend of video game adaptations
that appealed to gamers, *Stay Alive* brought gaming technology into a more fearful light,
which created a mixture of both technophobic and technophilic video game horror films
in the year 2006. However, unlike the films described in Chapter 2, *Stay Alive* does not
seem to be concerned with the damage that video game technology may cause, but the
damage it has already done. The use of Internet and videogame technology was already
widespread and accepted by the American masses, and *Stay Alive* was released at a time
when video game consoles were saturating the marketplace. The world that *Stay Alive*

---

[80] Roger Ebert, Rev. of *Silent Hill*, RogerEbert.Com. 21 Apr. 2006. 8 Apr. 2007
<http://rogerebert.suntimes.com/apps/pbcs.dll/article?AID=/20060420/REVIEWS/60421001/1023>.

creates with digital games being an unstoppable force may indeed be referring to the 2006 climate in which games have been accepted as a legitimate medium, even to the point that films such as *Bloodrayne* and *Silent Hill* celebrate them on the big screen.

This study has established that horror films were released in the 1990s to reference the anxieties and worries directed at the relatively new and unknown video game technologies. However, it has also established a shift beginning in 2000 in which horror films served to no longer vilify video games, but celebrate their existence and popularity in society. The release of *Stay Alive* in 2006 breaks this trend of game-friendly horror, which leads to the question of whether or not films will once again capitalize on a sense of hostility towards the changing video game technology. It is quite possible that other films may follow in the footsteps of *Stay Alive* and address current anxieties concerning the power that video games may have on the human mind. However, it is also possible that such technophobic films may be released in response to similar films that have succeeded in the box office.

Since the beginning of the new millennium, popular Hollywood horror films have vilified not only video games, but various technological mediums. One example is *The Ring* (2002), which portrays a cursed video tape that, like the video game in *Stay Alive*, is made and distributed by a vengeful ghost to kill anyone who watches it. Another example is *Pulse* (2006), which depicts the Internet and desktop computers as sources of evil. It is entirely possible that *Stay Alive* is simply part of a trend of other horror films in the new millennium that emphasize, not just the fear of video games, but all forms of new

71

media technology. If this trend continues, video games could be vilified again on the big

screen along with other cutting edge technologies.

In addition to video game films of a technophobic nature, the film industry will

also likely continue the trend of glorifying and embodying the video game medium

through adaptations due to the continuing success of video game technology. *Bloodrayne*

and *Silent Hill* were two adaptation films released in 2006, and the future only promises

more of them. While this study is being written in 2007, another installment of the

Resident Evil franchise is slated for a fall release titled *Resident Evil: Extinction*. Video

game adaptation auteur Uwe Boll is also slated to release *Seed, Postal, Dungeon Siege,*

and a sequel to *Bloodrayne*, all of these being based on popular games.

While video game films of a technophobic nature and adaptations may continue to

be produced, there still remains the question as to why they are produced and how

popular technology affects their existence. Horror films have historically articulated

social concerns at the time of their production. [81] This study as a whole analyzes horror

films pertaining to video games which articulate America's fear and concern with this

technology, but also how this fear can change or diminish over time in response to

changing attitudes in popular culture. The video game horror films produced after 2000

have primarily done away with these fears because video games have proven to be

popular and lucrative amongst consumers and video game companies. The current

marketplace consists of powerful corporations competing on a regular basis to create the

latest and greatest video game consoles, and the consumers continue to purchase them.

[81] Andrew Tudor, "Why Horror? The Peculiar Pleasures of a Popular Genre," Horror: the
Film Reader. Ed. Mark Jancovich. (New York: Routledge, 2002) 50.

Thanks to the convergence of media, video games have even made it out of the domestic space and onto other devices such as cellular phones and MP3 players, making their presence even more recognizable to consumers. With the video game medium continuing to rise in popularity, the period of strongly fearing this new technology has passed, and it is inevitable that the film medium will continue to merge closer with the popular video game medium to appease not just moviegoers, but a completely different set of viewers devoted to contemporary game play.

In addition to these adaptations, there is still the previously-mentioned probability of films which will vilify technology within the diegesis. It is likely that horror films will continue to play upon the technophobic attitudes of moviegoers towards other relatively new and unknown technologies. While video game technology influenced the films of Chapter 2, other films have utilized the same storytelling method with other technologies. One example is the Internet, which has inspired various horror films including *Cry Wolf* (2005), *Hard Candy* (2006), and the previously-mentioned *Pulse* (2006). These are films that have depicted the Internet as the catalyst for horror within of diegetic frameworks of their narratives. Movie-goers and Hollywood may have accepted and become desensitized to video game technology, and this may continue to support the prominence of video game adaptation films. However, this does not dismiss the idea that new technologies will always exist, and will always give its users a feeling of uncertainty upon experiencing them for the first time. Therefore, horror films could always give their viewers something to fear in this technologically-evolving landscape of popular culture.

As a whole, this study observes the presence of technophobia in horror films, and how these fears may diminish or change over time in response to society's positive or negative feelings toward certain technologies. In this particular instance, video games represent that certain technology. By following the presence of video games in horror films released during the last two decades, it is observed that these films went from primarily fearing video games to primarily celebrating them. It was difficult for some people to gauge the unhealthy, immersive, or distracting side effects that came with playing these games, but over time they became entertainment staples, and were as accepted as a means of entertainment as cable television. The releases of these films happened to parallel American culture's shift from becoming first acquainted with a boom in video game technology, to becoming comfortable with and accustomed to the technology. While these films reflect society's feelings toward video game technology specifically, they also essentially reflect society's feelings toward any new technology. With constant innovations and breakthroughs, America will always feel a sense of hostility or anxiety toward a brand new technology. What these new technologies will be is unknown at the moment. However, Hollywood will likely be there to make a horror film about it.

Bibliography

Allen, Robert C., and Douglas Gomery. <u>Film History: Theory and Practice</u>. New York: Knopf, 1985.

Berger, Arthur A. <u>Video Games: a Popular Culture Phenomenon</u>. New Brunswick, NJ: Transaction, 2002.

Boll, Uwe. "Into the Dark: Behind the Scenes of *Alone in the Dark*." <u>Alone in the Dark</u> Dir. Uwe Boll. Perf. Christian Slater, Tara Reid, and Stephen Dorff. DVD. Lion's Gate Films, 2005.

Boll, Uwe. "Commentary Track." <u>House of the Dead</u>. Dir. Uwe Boll. Perf. Jonathan Cherry, Clint Howard, and Jurgen Prochnow. DVD. Artisan, 2003.

Bolter, Jay D., and Richard Grusin. <u>Remediation: Understanding New Media</u>. Cambridge, MA: The MIT P, 1999.

Bordwell, David, and Kristin Thompson. <u>Film History: an Introduction</u>. 2nd ed. New York: McGraw Hill, 2003.

Brown, Scott. "House of the Dead." <u>Entertainment Weekly.</u> 10 Oct. 2003. 20 May 2006 <http://www.ew.com/ew/article/review/movie/0,6115,485226~1~0~houseofdead, 00.html>.

Carroll, Noel. "Why Horror?" <u>Horror: the Film Reader</u>. Ed. Mark Jancovich. New York: Routledge, 2002. 33-47.

Darley, Andrew. <u>Visual Digital Culture: Surface Play and Spectacle in New Media Genres</u>. New York: Routledge, 2000.

Degrandpre, Richard. <u>Digitopia: the Look of the New Digital You</u>. New York: AtRandom.Com Books, 2001.

Dinello, Daniel. <u>Technophobia!: Science Fiction Visions of Posthuman Technology.</u> Austin, TX: University of Texas Press, 2005.

Ebert, Roger. Rev. of *Brainscan*. <u>RogerEbert.Com</u>. 22 Apr. 1994. 12 Apr. 2007 <http://rogerebert.suntimes.com/apps/pbcs.dll/article?AID=/19940422/REVIEWS /404220303/1023>.

Ebert, Roger. Rev. of *Doom*. <u>RogerEbert.com.</u> 21 Oct. 2005. 20 May 2006
    <http://rogerebert.suntimes.com/apps/pbcs.dll/article?AID=/20051020/REVIEWS
    /51012003/1023>.

Ebert, Roger. Rev. of *Silent Hill*, <u>RogerEbert.Com</u>. 21 Apr. 2006. 8 Apr. 2007
    <http://rogerebert.suntimes.com/apps/pbcs.dll/article?AID=/20060420/REVIEWS
    /60421001/1023>.

Elsaesser, Thomas, and Warren Buckland. <u>Studying Contemporary American Film</u>.
    London: Arnold, 2002.

Grodal, Torben. "Stories for Eye, Ear, and Muscles: Video Games, Media, and Embodied
    Experiences." <u>The Video Game Theory Reader</u>. Ed. Mark J. Wolf and Bernard
    Perron. New York: Routledge, 2003. 129-157.

Hand, Richard J. "Proliferating Horrors: Survival Horror and the Resident Evil
    Franchise." <u>Horror Film: Creating and Marketing Fear</u>. Ed. Steffen Hantke.
    Jackson: University Press of Mississippi, 2004. 117-135.

Harrington, Richard. "The Lawnmower Man." <u>The Washington Post</u> 7 Mar. 2007. 12
    Apr. 2007 <http://www.washingtonpost.com/wp-
    srv/style/longterm/movies/videos/thelawnmowermanrharrington_a0ab25.htm>

Jenkins, Henry. <u>Convergence Culture: Where Old and New Media Collide</u>. New York:
    New York UP, 2006.

Keane, Steve. "From Hardware to Fleshware: Plugging into David Cronenberg's
    EXistenZ." <u>ScreenPlay: Cinema/videogames/interfaces</u>. Eds. Geoff King and
    Tanya Krzywinska. London: Wallflower Press, 2002. 145-157.

Kerr, Aphra. "The Business of Making Digital Games." <u>Understanding Digital Games</u>.
    Ed. Jason Rutter and Jo Bryce. Thousand Oaks, CA: Sage Publications, 2006. 36-
    58.

King, Geoff. <u>Spectacular Narratives: Hollywood in the Age of the Blockbuster</u>. New
    York: I.B. Tauris, 2000.

King, Geoff, and Tanya Krzywinska. "Film Studies and Digital Games." <u>Understanding
    Digital Games</u>. Ed. Jason Rutter and Jo Bryce. Thousand Oaks, CA: Sage
    Publications, 2006. 112-128.

Kirriemuir, John. "A History of Digital Games." <u>Understanding Digital Games</u>. Ed. Jason
    Rutter and Jo Bryce. Thousand Oaks, CA: Sage Publications, 2006. 21-36.

Kline, Stephen, Nick Dyer-Witheford, and Greig De Peuter. <u>Digital Play: the Interaction of Technology, Culture, and Marketing</u>. Quebec: McGill-Queen's UP, 2003.

Krzywinska, Tanya. "Hands-On Horror." <u>ScreenPlay: Cinema/videogames/interfaces</u>. Eds. Geoff King and Tanya Krzywinska. London: Wallflower Press, 2002. 206-225.

Lewis, Peter H. "The Summer Report: Ex Machina; Child's Play." <u>The New York Times</u> 6 Aug. 1989. 12 Apr. 2007 <http://select.nytimes.com>.

Mastai, Elan. "Into the Dark: Behind the Scenes of *Alone in the Dark*." <u>Alone in the Dark</u> Dir. Uwe Boll. Perf. Christian Slater, Tara Reid, and Stephen Dorff. DVD. Lion's Gate Films, 2005.

McMahan, Alison. "Immersion, Engagement, and Presence: a Method for Analyzing 3-D Video Games." <u>The Video Game Theory Reader</u>. Ed. Mark J. Wolf and Bernard Perron. New York: Routledge, 2003. 67-87.

Montesano, Anthony P. "CD-ROM 'Trickster' Treat: Brainscan." <u>Cinefantastique</u> 25 (1994): 48-51.

Morris, Sue. "First-Person Shooters: the Game Apparatus." <u>Screenplay: Cinema/Videogames/Interfaces</u>. Ed. Geoff King and Tanya Krzywinska. London: Wallflower P, 2002. 81-98.

Morris, Wesley. "'Bloodrayne' Fun Comes in Spurts." <u>Boston Globe</u> 7 Jan. 2006. 8 Apr. 2007 <http://www.boston.com/ae/movies/articles/2006/01/07/bloodrayne_fun_comes_in_spurts/>.

Murray, Janet. "From Game-Story to Cyberdrama." <u>First Person</u>. Ed. Noah Wardrip-Fruin and Pat Harrigan. Cambridge, MA: The MIT P, 2004. 2-11.

Pollack, Andrew. "Tech Notes; All Aboard for Virtuality." <u>The New York Times</u> 5 Jan. 1992. 12 Apr. 2007 <http://select.nytimes.com>.

Pomerance, Murray. "Neither Here Nor There: Existenz as "Elevator Film"" <u>Quarterly Review of Film and Video</u> 20 (2003): 1-14.

Poole, Steven. <u>Trigger Happy: Videogames and the Entertainment Revolution</u>. New York: Arcade, 2000.

Sobchack, Vivian. <u>Screening Space: the American Science Fiction Film</u>. 2nd ed. New York City: Ungar Company, 1993.

Tudor, Andrew. "Why Horror? the Peculiar Pleasures of a Popular Genre." <u>Horror: the Film Reader</u>. Ed. Mark Jancovich. New York: Routledge, 2002. 47-57.

Waller, Gregory. <u>American Horrors</u>. Chicago and Urbana: University of Illinois Press, 1987.

Williams, Dmitri. "The Video Game Ligtning Rod: Constructions of a New Technology, 1970-2000." <u>Information, Communication, & Society</u> 6 (2003): 523-550.

Williams, Linda. "Film Bodies: Gender, Genre, and Excess." <u>Film Theory and Criticism: Introductory Readings</u>. 5th ed. Ed. Leo Braudy and Marshall Cohen. New York: Oxford UP, 1999. 701-716.

Printed in the United Kingdom
by Lightning Source UK Ltd.
128334UK00001B/2/P